Wisdom of the Galactics

Channeled Messages to Elevate Your Life

Dr. Lisa Thompson

As You Wish Publishing, LLC
Phoenix, AZ

Cover photography: Ashton Miyako
Cover design by: As You Wish Publishing
Interior design by: As You Wish Publishing
Author portrait by: Ashton Miyako
Drawing of Arcturian Uluru with Lisa: Tiffany Guinn

ISBN: 978-1-951131-62-3

www.DrLisaJThompson.com

Contents

Chapter 1

Calling in the Energy and Wisdom of the Galactics

"We come in love. We wish to help humanity wake up, to let go of fear and judgment. We are here to remind you of who and what you are and where you come from. Expand your mind, your reality. Allow in new levels of understanding and integration." — Arcturian Uluru, Connection to the Cosmos: Remembering Your Galactic Heritage and Embracing Your Oneness

My connection to my galactic family and guides has been ongoing over the last several years. Each time I consciously call in their support and guidance, the relationship deepens. One of my missions as a Galactic Ambassador is to help bridge the gap between those on Earth ready to meet their family and guides and those residing in higher dimensional reality, whether here on Earth or beyond.

Early in 2023, my higher dimensional team asked me to step out of my comfort zone and move into new territory, trusting them to teach through me via channeling. Although I had been channeling the Arcturians for the last year, I had yet to channel other groups. They had me focus on 13 different extraterrestrial and extradimensional races to which I felt a personal connection. After writing down the names of these races, I put together a 14-week series of sessions to call in their energy and wisdom each week, focusing on a different group. The first session of the series was a general overview of these groups and an initial meeting of them in a guided meditative journey.

My team did not let me know what would happen in these sessions, as they wanted me to release my control. Still, they did share some of the energy and wisdom that would come through each race ahead of time. I was to trust that I could move my ego aside and let them teach through me.

The information I share in this book comes directly from these sessions. Each chapter gives an overview of who the galactic group is, what they may look like, and how they relate to Earth. I include information about some of the different crystals/stones that can help you to connect deeper to each group. There are journaling prompts before and after the transcribed meditative journey. The meditative journey each group channeled was transcribed from the audio and has only been slightly edited for grammar. I wanted to keep the integrity and flavor of the messages as pure as possible for each group.

As you read the journey for each group, allow your mind to follow the words so you can experience the energy coming from the transmission. The sessions have been recorded, so I offer those separately, should you desire to experience them first-hand. I have also edited down the recorded material to a stand-alone meditative journey for each group that ranges from 35-55 minutes each.

The recorded sessions include crystal singing bowls to help usher in the energy and frequency of the themes for each session. The video replays and stand-alone meditative journeys are available for purchase on my website at www.DrLisaJThompson.com.

A Brief History of My Extraterrestrial Experiences

I grew up in an esoteric, metaphysical, spiritual household. My mother became an Astrologer when I was two years old, after divorcing my father and moving us to Oklahoma City, Oklahoma, from Colorado. My mom's friends all practiced metaphysical science, including astrology, numerology, tarot, and witchcraft. As a single mom, she brought me to her nighttime astrology classes. She would also take me to her favorite metaphysical gift and bookstore, Starwind, where I would look at the crystals and smell the essential oils. I enjoyed the energy of the store.

My mother and aunt were introduced to Ramtha, a channeled entity who speaks through JZ Knight, in 1985, through tapes and videos. They attended an in-person weekend seminar in early 1986 in Denver, Colorado, called "The Days to Come." The information shared in that seminar included future predictions of severe drought, continuous natural disasters, the rise of the oceans, and the collapse of the financial system. It was suggested to those attending the event to create a life of sovereignty by living off the land in an area with abundant rainfall.

After that weekend, my mom and aunt decided we could no longer safely live in Oklahoma. They felt the need to live in a "safer" place where they could grow their own food and have more water supply. After some exploration, they decided on Washington state, where JZ Knight resided and did most of her channeling. In the summer of 1986, we moved from Oklahoma to Washington just outside Olympia, the state capitol.

I was 13 years old and getting ready to start eighth grade.

I was hesitant to participate in the teachings of Ramtha at first. The concept of channeling was strange to me, and I didn't understand it. After attending my first event, a personal Question and Answer session with only 100 people in attendance, I knew that Ramtha was an actual entity and JZ Knight was not acting. I could feel the energy coming out of the body as Ramtha/JZ walked around the space to address the audience. It was different than anything I had ever experienced. I participated in various events over the next few years where we learned concepts of creating our reality, being one with Source, understanding higher dimensional beings, and so much more. One event excited me. It was on the topic of extraterrestrials. While I don't remember the details of what we learned in that session, it confirmed my belief that extraterrestrials were real. In other sessions, we learned about other "mythical" creatures being real, including faeries, dragons, sasquatch, unicorns, and others.

At 15, I had my first conscious experience of being taken onto a spacecraft. I write more about this experience in my book, Connection to the Cosmos: Remembering Your Galactic Heritage and Embracing Your Oneness. In this instance, I was taken to Io, one of Jupiter's moons, where there was a small colony inside of the moon of an undetermined extraterrestrial race. Those of us that were brought there were being tested to see if something happened to Earth if we could live in an environment like that or similar. This experience was in 1988; we were still in the Cold War and on the verge of World War 3. There was a genuine timeline where something could have destroyed the Earth.

For a few months after the experience, I thought it was just a dream. What I understand now is that with dreams, we tend to forget details within the first 10 minutes of waking up. I didn't forget. A few months later, I was reading Whitley Strieber's book, *Communion*. The group I had been taken by differed from Strieber's experience with gray extraterrestrials. At the end of his book, he interviewed different people that had been taken. They all shared a similar experience to him of being with gray extraterrestrials. There was one exception of a man who had a completely different story. He told Strieber he had been taken to a moon of Jupiter and told he was one of the chosen ones. Strieber made a side comment about it, hoping it wasn't Io. When I read that statement, I had head-to-toe chills through my body, and tears started coming down my face. That was my body's way of saying it was a real experience. It was not a dream.

Knowing she would believe me, I immediately told my mother about the experience. That week, she introduced me to one of the students in the Ramtha School who had formerly been a very high government official who knew about the different extraterrestrial races that our government knows about and works with. I told him my story, and although he didn't know the race I described, he validated that it was a real experience.

Being able to remember the experience and having it validated as a teenager was genuinely life-changing. I didn't have to go through my life thinking I was crazy or making it up. It planted the seed for the work I do now as a Galactic Ambassador and Channeler. I discovered only a couple of years ago that I had been with this same group multiple times throughout my childhood. I was only allowed to remember my experience because I was mature enough to understand the situation, and the opportunity to have it validated was present.

At 16, I decided I had learned enough from Ramtha for the time being, and I wanted to have a "normal" life to fit in with my peers. It was not easy being a "Ramster" (common nickname of students of Ramtha) in our town, which was highly polarized with an us versus them mentality. The town only had about 2,000 residents but over 20 different churches.

At the age of 28 (in December of 2000), after earning my PhD in Evolutionary Biology from the University of Chicago and the Field Museum of Natural History,

I was reintroduced to the teachings of Ramtha by my mother's chiropractor. He thought I would appreciate the new content of teachings, which focused on understanding quantum mechanics, brain physiology, and other non-mainstream types of science that helped to explain what we were learning at the spiritual level.

While participating in the Ramtha School, I had numerous experiences outside of third-dimensional, physical reality. I witnessed countless spacecraft, orbs, and plasma. I had moments of understanding my genuine connection to Source. I was consciously creating my reality. Although I left the Ramtha School in the spring of 2006, I carried the teachings and experiences with me.

Meeting Arcturian Uluru and Others

In October 2018, I took a weekly psychic/intuition class that lasted several months. On the first night of class, our teacher, Lisa Holm, led us through a meditative journey to meet a spirit guide who would help us get extra information if we needed it. In this journey, I went to a completely different realm, standing before a small group of blue-skinned beings. They had larger heads, no hair, large eyes, and skinny bodies. They exuded the purest love I have ever felt – so much beyond this Earth reality. Although there were several of them, one acted as the spokesperson. The message they had for me came through telepathy: "You are one of us. We are one of you. We are family." I was given a gift of a clear quartz crystal, which I didn't understand the meaning of at that time. When I asked if they had a name they wanted to be called, I was given the name Uluru.

I had no idea who they were as I came out of this journey. Each classmate shared who their spirit guide was. I was the only one to share about a non-human guide. One of my classmates knew some of the different extraterrestrial groups who were known, and based on my description, she thought it was either the Blue Avians or the Arcturians. I went home to Google who those two groups were. As soon as I saw the images of the Arcturians, I knew that was who I met.

Over the last several years, I have come to understand my relation to the Arcturians. Uluru is the aspect of me as an Arcturian. I am Uluru. When I discovered I had this connection, it allowed the eventual channeling of Uluru to flow much easier through me.

During the months of taking the psychic/intuition class, I met Andromedans and Blue Avians. In the last few years, I have worked with the energy of the Mantis, Zetas, Pleiadians, and others. In 2022, I discovered my connection to the Agarthans (Inner Earth beings) and being a merperson on a water planet in the Sirius star system during an Ascension session with my friend Tracey Mahan. I also had a QHHT session where I remembered my life as a being from Sirius, interacting with Earth during ancient Egypt and the construction of the pyramids. In this life, I was a genetic engineer helping to modify and upgrade the DNA of Earth humans. We did this by emitting a specific sound frequency from our spacecraft.

During a channeled session with Daniel Scranton in the summer of 2023, I confirmed that I am part of the Zeta-human hybrid program and other hybrid programs that are not as well known. I have 12 hybrid children from the Zeta program who I hope to meet physically one day. I know I volunteered for this enthusiastically.

The realization that Uluru was me led me to know that these other groups I was inspired and guided to teach about are also just aspects of me. I have parallel lives as each of these 13 galactic races. This allows me to tap into their energy more quickly and to trust what is coming through is from a higher dimensional reality. I only call forth entities in the fifth dimension and higher, which I explain in the next chapter. The deeper I understand my connection and relationship to these groups, the more I realize I am much more non-Earth-based than of this Earth.

Galactic Race Overview

There are specific themes I have elicited from each of the 13 groups. As you will discover, some groups have overlapping qualities and wisdom. Some of the extraterrestrials actively work together in the higher realms for a common cause. Although I have specific wisdom coming through as I channel, please understand that there is so much more that each group has to offer. I invite you to pick one group that you are called to understand and work with that energy. Once you integrate their energy and wisdom into your life, you may be called to get to know a second group. This is not something to be rushed. When you start paying attention to what the energy feels like, you can begin to distinguish between the different groups as they come through you.

As you work with these different groups, I invite you to tune in to your specific connection to them. Like me, each of you may have lives as some or all of these beings. There may be groups that you resonate with strongly. The more you stay open to what each group can usher in for you, the deeper your connection will be to all conscious beings. Countless other groups exist beyond the scope of this book. I invite you to use this as an introduction and starting point to discover who you really are.

One way to use this material is to read through the entire book to get an overview and flavor of each group. Once you know which group you are most called to understand more deeply, you can practice calling in their energy. You may also use the *Wisdom of the Galactics Oracle Deck* I have created to guide you into which group and message you most need to understand at that moment. As mentioned, the transcribed journeys in each section of this book are voice-recorded. The recorded journeys and the Oracle Deck can be acquired on my website at www.DrLisaJThompson.com.

The galactic group chapters are arranged alphabetically, making navigating easier when used as a resource. Below is a breakdown of the themes and wisdom for each of the 13 galactic groups.

Agarthan Wisdom

Balance
Community
Harmony
Nature

Andromedan Wisdom

Peace
Freedom

Justice

Evolution

Arcturian Wisdom

Emotional Healing

Love

Unity

Creativity

Blue Avian Wisdom

Consciousness

Expansion

Nurture

Vibration

Hybrid Wisdom

Choice

Clarity

Manifestation

Release

Lyran Wisdom

Adventure

Fearless

Independent

Self-worth

Mantis Wisdom

Ancient Wisdom
Creation
Divine Masculine
Master Healing

Orion Wisdom

Equality
Higher perspective
Inspiration
Integration

Pleiadian Wisdom

Compassion
Divine Feminine
Empathy
Growth

Reptilian Wisdom

Adaptability
Confident
Self-Power
Transformation

Sirian Wisdom

Ascension
Joy

Physical healing
Playful

Vegan Wisdom

Faith
Inner wisdom
Introspection
Meditation

Zeta Wisdom

Neutrality
Observe
Perception
Timeline

In the next chapter, Arcturian Uluru shares a welcome message. I explain the different dimensions and densities for you to understand why you want to work with higher vibrational beings. I lead you through a process that helps to raise your vibration to connect to these higher dimensional beings.

Stay curious and open-minded as you explore each group.

Chapter 2

Raising Your Vibration

Channeled Message from Arcturian Uluru

"We are the Arcturians. We come in love and peace. We are so very happy that you joined us on this journey. You have so many beau-

tiful guides that want to work with you. We appreciate your willingness to be here to meet them, to connect with them. We want you to know they want to connect with you. They want to share their energy and wisdom. They love you so very much, as do we. Those of us in the higher dimensional realities understand things from a much higher perspective. We can share our wisdom and our energy with you.

Sometimes it's very hard to live on that Earth plane, that polarized plane. We want you to understand there is so much more beyond the polarization. There is love. There is unity. There is no judgment. We ask that you first and foremost get over the judgment of your-self. When you are able to stop your self-judg-ment, you are able to then let go of judg-ment of other people and understand that everyone is coming from their own perspec-tive, their own wisdom. Some have awakened. Some have evolved a little bit more than oth-ers. That is perfectly fine because there is no time. There is no past. There is no future. All timelines exist simultaneously.

We want you to understand that even in your Earth reality, you have the ability to choose which timeline you want to be in. How we advise you to do this is we want you to imagine all timelines stacked on top of each other in parallel. We want you to imagine, to envision, to feel the emotion of the reality that you most want in your life. The more that you can hold this focus and the energy as if it already is so, it is already your reality. The more that you hold the emotion, the vision, then you will shift into that timeline naturally. No matter what is going on around you and the low-vibration things going on Earth, you can stay above it. You can experience a completely different reality. You have already done it at different times in your life, and you didn't even know it. The more conscious that you can be in doing this practice, the more joy, the more passion, the more love you're going to have in your life.

We ask you to stay in as high a vibration as you can throughout your day because you are a frequency-specific energy. Everyone, every being, is frequency specific. What that means is that the higher the frequency that you carry, you are going to have that matched in the people and the beings that come into your life. When you are vibrating in this high state, you will only experience high vibe beings coming in. Lower vibes cannot penetrate this. They are repelled. They cannot match that frequency.

We know it is hard on your Earth. You sometimes get in that negative state, that polarized state. You pay attention to the news, the media, and all of the bad stuff going on. That is but one timeline, one existence. Yes, that doesn't mean that it's not happening in other timelines, but it does not have to affect you. You have a choice. You have full choice in creating what reality you want to experience. We invite you to do this. The more you can practice being in the high vibration, keeping your focus, and feeling it in your body as if it has already happened, you will shift naturally. Thank you very much for allowing us to share this brief message with you. We love you so very much."

Dimensional & Density Frequencies

The groups we work with in these sessions are multi-dimensional, just as you are. Each group has its unique history of evolution, which I will briefly cover in each chapter. I invite you to stay as open-minded as you tune into the energy of each group, as you may be surprised. We are only calling in those beings that reside in higher dimensional reality. There is absolutely nothing to fear. You are always in control over what you experience and how you perceive it.

Earth humans primarily reside in third and fourth-dimensional reality, also called third density. Occasionally, there is a shift into low fifth-dimensional reality, but that isn't sustainable for most humans at this time. We are evolving as a race to live permanently in fifth-dimensional reality, also known as fourth density. This most commonly is referred to as 5D.

Polarity is the experience of the third and fourth dimensions, where there is a perception of good/bad, positive/negative, and black/white. As we move into the fifth dimension, the polarity disintegrates, and the judgment disappears. The higher in vibration/frequency that we go, the polarity disappears altogether, and we become more of a collective consciousness, with the understanding that we are all one. We are all connected.

There are extraterrestrial races who reside in third and fourth-dimensional reality, as humans do. They also experience polarity. Some individuals of these races are more oriented to "service to self," while others are more oriented to "service to others." We cannot lump all individuals of a race into a positive or negative polarization, just as we can't do that with humans on Earth. It's important to note that there are also multiple races of beings within the general categories of grays and reptilians who come from different star systems. Some people in the Ufology world throw these terms around without being specific to the actual type of gray or reptilian.

The 13 galactic groups called into this environment within the book, and the recorded sessions reside in the fifth dimension and higher. We must raise our vibration to connect with beings who reside in a much higher frequency. When we do this and consciously ask for connection, these beings can lower their vibration to have a common ground to communicate with. We do this as an inward journey rather than an outward physical experience. The following transcription is an example of a process I use to raise my vibration and those of my clients and students. Feel free to use this and modify it as desired to get yourself into a higher vibrational state.

Journey to Raise Vibration

Go ahead and close your eyes. Get as comfortable into the seat or bed you're sitting or lying on. Shift your body so you can fully relax, knowing you are in total control of this journey. You're in total control of the experience. You are safe. Only that energy which is of the highest vibration, of love, is allowed to come into your space today. Above your head, I want you to imagine a beautiful white sparkling light - Source light energy. Imagine this white sparkling light falling down over your body like a waterfall, from your head down to your feet, moving into the center of the Earth. Keep running this white sparkling, shimmering light from your head down to your feet into the center of the Earth. As this white light moves over your body, it's removing tension from your surface muscles.

Now, I want you to open the top of your head, your crown chakra. Allow this white light energy to come down into your head, moving down through your body, down through your legs, and out through the bottom of your feet into the center of the Earth. Visualize this beautiful white shimmering light pouring into the top of your head, moving behind your eyes, into your jaw, your neck, your shoulders and arms, down through your chest, your belly, your hips, and down through your legs and out through the bottom of your feet into the center of the Earth. As this white light moves through your body like a river, it's clearing away the debris. It's removing the blockages. It's shining light in all of the dark places. It's releasing any tension, any stuck energy in your body, breaking through that and turning it into tiny particles to move out through the bottom of your feet into the center of the Earth. Allow your body to relax deeper. Allow your body to feel lighter and lighter as you're running this white light energy, raising your vibration.

We're going to do a very quick balancing of the chakras to let this energy flow even stronger. Starting at the root chakra, the base of your spine, see red spinning energy, spinning freely, easily. Move up now to your sacral, just a couple of inches below your naval, and see orange spinning energy. It's spinning in perfect harmony with the red below it. Move up now to the solar plexus, the belly, and see yellow spinning energy. The yellow is spinning in perfect harmony with the orange and the red. Move up now to your heart and see green spinning energy. The green is spinning in perfect harmony with the yellow, the orange, and the red. Move now to your throat and see blue spinning energy. The blue is spinning in perfect harmony with the green, the yellow, the orange, and the red. Move up now to your third eye, in the center of your forehead, and see indigo spinning energy. The indigo is spinning in harmony with the blue, the green, the yellow, the orange, and the red. Move up now to your crown chakra and see violet spinning energy. The violet is spinning in perfect harmony with the indigo, the blue, the green, the yellow, the orange, and the red.

From an observer's perspective, now see all of these energy centers spinning in perfect harmony with each other, lit up like a rainbow, and energy flowing easily up and down the spinal column. Everything is flowing easily through your body. Once again, open the top of your head and allow the white light energy to come back in through the top of your head, moving down very easily now through the body, releasing any remaining tension or blockages, down through your feet and out into the center of the Earth. Open up your root chakra and allow the white light energy that's been recycled in the center of the Earth to come back up through the root, meeting the light from above in the heart space. The light from above meets the light from below, intertwining together in the heart.

In this heart chakra space, once again, see the green spinning energy. Expand that green energy beyond your body. Expand it out beyond your room, beyond your house. Expand the green energy as far out into time, space, and dimension as you can imagine. You're sending out love energy, the universal law, the universal language. Only that which is of love is allowed to come into your space today for your highest and greatest good. Resonating in the energy of love, bring that love back in. Bring the green energy back into your body.

I want you to imagine your body as vibrating cells, trillions of golden cells, vibrating together in perfect harmony. Go inside one of those cells. Go inside the nucleus to where the DNA resides. Imagine the double helix spiral of the DNA, the spiral ladder. You're intuitively now going to the part of the DNA ready to be activated today to deepen your connection with your galactic family and guides, to your higher self, your higher being. See the DNA splitting apart. The rungs of the ladder are splitting apart, and a flash of golden white energy is blasting through the center where it's open, activating the DNA right now. Close the DNA. Pull yourself out of the nucleus and out of the cell. Once again, see your body as vibrating cells, trillions of cells. Imagine those cells vibrating faster and faster and faster. They vibrate together so fast that they blur together to create a golden energy body, raising your frequency and vibration. You are ready to meet the galactic guides coming today to be with you.

Now that you understand how to raise your vibration, it's time to dive deeply into each group. Enjoy the ride!

Chapter 3

Agarthans

Who are the Agarthans?

The Agarthans are a specific race of human-like beings that reside within Inner Earth. Because they live within Earth, they are not technically extraterrestrials. Instead, they are extradimensional, living outside third and fourth-dimensional reality. Although different races reside within Inner Earth, the Agarthans appear Nordic. They generally have light skin, white or fair hair, and light eyes. This appearance may be an adaptation to their subterranean world, as they don't experience the same UV radiation that we have on the surface of Earth. They are a spiritually advanced race of beings operating in a primarily fifth-dimensional reality.

Agarthans reside in different communities and cities around the globe, connected by tunnels. Some of these communities include the city of Telos within Mount

Shasta, Shambhala (also known as Shangri-La) in Asia, and Catharia underneath the Aegean Sea. The north and south poles are known entrance and exit points, as documented by Admiral Richard Byrd during expeditions he made in the early 1900's. Additional portals to Inner Earth are within volcanoes, cave and tunnel systems, and deep in the oceans and lakes worldwide.

The Agarthans developed as a separate group from surface-dwelling humans just before the destruction of Atlantis and Lemuria. As the Lemurian continent was on the brink of collapse due to war with Atlantis, a group of spiritually advanced Lemurians went inside of the Earth. In addition, a group of humans from Atlantis, the positive priests and priestesses, went underground before the destruction. The Lemurian and Atlantis groups created a dynamic civilization within the Earth, and they are now collectively referred to as the Agarthans.

There are a few individual Agarthans that have regular contact with some humans. Ascended master Saint Germain lives within Telos. There are numerous stories of people encountering him when they visited Mount Shasta, including one of my very good friends, Pamelah. Ka Aree is a well-known high priestess of Inner Earth. Master Adama is another known Agarthan who people often connect with.

Some Agarthans come to the surface of Earth to get a sense of the state of the external Earth. They travel in spaceships, which have been seen moving in and out of volcanoes and in and out of the water. They help to hold the energy balance of Mother Gaia from the inside, just as many surface humans hold the energy balance from above. To interact with Agarthans, one must shift into a fifth-dimensional consciousness. In rare interactions, some Agarthans lower their vibration to third density to interact with humans on the surface.

During a parallel life regression session in 2022, my client had an unexpected encounter with a male Agarthan named John, who showed her what his part of Inner Earth looked like. He shared beautiful information. The client described seeing a lot of vegetation with advanced technology in complete harmony with the environment. John told her that their nutrition comes primarily from berries, and their lifespan is approximately 900 years.

The message below is part of the transcription from this session:

Lisa: Are they able to show themselves to humans on the surface?

Client: They do all the time.

Lisa: What is their purpose for doing that?

Client: To have contact. To have ambassadors because sometimes, with Earth, people don't know what to think anymore, and so much has been distorted. So, we need ambassadors to keep the message, some of this truth, the history, alive. We need that. Otherwise, people of the Earth would be so lost.

Lisa: What do they want us humans to know?

Client: That they are loved, and now being a light isn't all there is. It's love. God is love. We are very conscious of our environment. We really take care of her, Mother Nature. The Earth is alive. It supports us. It gives us oxygen, everything around us. This is technology that you don't quite understand, but you need to know the plant pays for everything on this Earth, plays its part. Everything plays a part. Stop destroying things. The ecosystem, it all works together, and that's why our technology is so.

Lisa: What is their understanding of spirituality?

Client: It's love. Everything around them is a form of spirituality: the plant, the water, people working together. It's a practice. It's a way of life, connecting with everything around you.

Lisa: Does John have any last things he would like to share?

Client: Stay connected. Stay connected to Source. Stay connected to us. You're part of something bigger. Always remember that. You're not alone in the Universe.

The energy and wisdom of the Agarthans include:

Balance

Community

Harmony

Nature

Stones/crystals to help you connect:

white jade, howlite, white crystal, and other white stones; green stones that represent nature and Earth (and any other stones that you are called to work with)

Journal prompt:

How much time do you spend in nature?

How would you describe your community?

Where could you use more harmony and balance in your life – relationships, work, personal?

Summary of the Agarthan Journey

In this session, the Agarthans take you on a journey to Inner Earth to explore their community and experience how they live. They are in complete harmony with each other and every living thing around them. Saint Germain invites you to experience the cleansing power of the violet flame.

The induction part of the journey to raise your vibration and activate your DNA has been omitted. Please refer to Chapter 2 for the process to get yourself into a higher vibrational state of mind.

Journey to Meet Your Agarthan

In front of you is a door. Walk over to the door, and on the other side of the door is a room with two chairs facing each other. Go ahead and open the door and move through the door. Walk towards one of the chairs and sit down. Across from you is another chair. Look over at the door and notice a gray shimmering mist starting to form around the door. That gray mist is getting thicker and thicker. It's twirling around, and through the door now is one or more of your Agarthans coming through the door to come and sit down in the chair in front of you.

Now, they are sitting down in front of you. Notice how many there are in the room. Notice what they look like. Are they all human type, or are they something different? There is no right or wrong. See the details of what they look like, the one that's sitting in the chair across from you. Look at their head. Look at their hair. What does their hair look like? What color is their hair? How long is it? Take a look at their face and look at their eyes. Are their eyes proportionate like human eyes? Are they bigger or smaller, or something different? What color are the eyes that you are looking into? Notice the details. Allow yourself to see this. Looking at their nose and their mouth, what do these look like? Take a look at their bodies. Are they wearing clothing or not? If they're wearing clothing, what do you see? What color is their clothing? How would you describe it? Notice what gender they might be. Are they male? Female? Perhaps androgynous?

Look deep into the eyes of the Agarthan sitting across from you. Receive a message that they came to bring you today. This message may come through words that they speak through their mouth. It may come through telepathy or images. Receive the message now.

They also brought a gift for you. Hold your hands out and receive the gift that they brought for you. You may already understand what it means and what it is. If not, receive the gift. Ask them what the purpose and meaning of this gift is for you today in this time and place. Receive that answer now. Thank them for the gift and the message.

Ask them if they have a name they would like to be called. Some of the names might be easy. Some of them are more challenging. Receive their name now if they have one to give you.

Now, once again, look into their eyes. They want to take you on a journey to where they live, a journey into Inner Earth for you to experience it first-hand, for you to know what kind of community they live in, and how they work together. There are multiple ways to journey to Inner Earth. You may simply see a portal and walk through it. Perhaps you ride a dragon down into Inner Earth. Or perhaps you take a spaceship, which will go into the water and one of the tunnels. Take your Agarthan's hand and walk over to the door. Walk through the door. You're going to have a choice of taking a portal, a dragon, a spaceship, or some other means of transporting to Inner Earth, knowing that you have the ability to do this.

Choose one of the options now. We're going through the tunnel, taking the journey. You may have already arrived. You may still be in the tunnel. Allow the root chakra frequency to carry you down deep inside the Earth, where you will emerge into one of the Inner Earth communities. It doesn't matter which one you go to. Trust yourself to take this journey through this tunnel now. You're starting to emerge out of the tunnel, and in front of you is a beautiful community. Notice the details of what it looks like inside of Inner Earth, where you have emerged. You may see something that has buildings in combination with nature. It may just be nature itself. It may be something completely different. Allow your Agarthan to give you a tour of this place that you have arrived at.

What do you notice about the sights? Take in the details of the sights that you're seeing. Perhaps there may be crystals or waterfalls. Where is the light source coming from? Is there an inner sun? Is there ambient light from some unknown source? Allow them to show you the details. I want you to see how they work together in the community. I want you to see how they govern from this higher dimensional reality without judgment of one another's ideas, having understanding for all sides, all perceptions of reality. Notice how in tune with nature they are, how they treat their environment, and how pristine this environment is. There are plenty of resources for every living being in this community. There is no scarcity. There is communal sharing, giving, and receiving. There are no power plays. While there still is a duality of gender, all are equal. No one is better than or lesser than. They are in balance with themselves, in balance with their bodies, in balance with each other, with their environment, with the plants and the animals, and all other life that surrounds them. They know every living thing has consciousness. Even the things that don't appear live, such as the rocks, have consciousness. The crystals have consciousness. Take all of this in. Let them guide you. Let them show you. Have this experience to understand what fifth-dimensional reality can be. What it is like? Let this frequency allow you to feel what they feel.

I want you to see yourself as one of them. See yourself as an Agarthan. Your body is starting to change form and coming in tune with all around you, becoming in tune with nature, the animals, the plants, the fungi, and all of nature surrounding you in this environment. Understand your relationship, your connection, doing no harm, being in balance, and appreciating what this nature provides for resources without overtaking them. Now, I want you, as an Agarthan, to experience where you would fit in in this community. I want you to experience, no matter what you choose, whatever your gifts that you're sharing with the community, that it is welcome. It is respected. All are equal. All have gifts to share. Feel the harmony and the balance of being part of this community, really experiencing the allowance of all ideas and all perceptions. There is no right or wrong. There is understanding. There is acceptance.

Now as you're still in this beautiful Inner Earth environment, you're going to walk over to the area where you see the violet flame. Walk over towards the violet flame and sit down in a very comfy chair where you can observe the violet flame in front of you. Next to this violet flame is Saint Germain standing there smiling at you, inviting you to look deep into this violet flame. Allow your mind to see this violet flame. As you're watching it flicker and dance, your mind is becoming one with the violet flame. As your mind becomes one, it's cleansing away all the negative emotions you've been carrying. It's releasing all the judgment. See this purple dancing in front of you, becoming part of it, allowing it to burn away all that does not serve you in this Earth human life. Allow yourself to rid yourself of these negative emotions so that you may maintain your fifth-dimensional vibration easier, longer, and more sustained. Understand the harmony of the community, the harmony of the Universe, being in balance, releasing any negativity that you've been holding on to. Let the purple flame, the violet flame, burn it all away.

Now, see yourself merging with this violet flame. As it surrounds your body, it's becoming one with your body. You are the violet. You are this higher vibrational energy. Observe your human self. See your human face inside of the flame. Observe yourself in this Earth life, inside the flame. Let it play like a movie in front of you. See yourself in your Earth human body, inside the flame. See yourself in nature, barefoot. Whether you're standing on the grass, the dirt, the soil, the sand, or the rock, feel your bare feet on the ground. See them on the ground.

This grounding helps you connect to nature. It helps you connect to higher dimensional reality. It enables you to maintain a higher state of vibration. Observe it now.

As you watch the flame, see your human-self building a beautiful, harmonious community. You may already have one; if you do, I want you to add to that community. If you don't have the community you would like, see yourself building community, one person at a time, perhaps groups at a time, whatever way you choose. Build a community of those who are equal in their frequency signature. Those not vibrating at the same frequency cannot be with you for long periods. See yourself in this high state of vibration, attracting your tribe, where you're able to vibrate together in high vibration. Create a beautiful, harmonious community of acceptance.

See how harmonious you are in all aspects of this human life: your relationships, work, and personal life. Every cell of your body is in harmony with the other cells, creating perfect health, longevity, and energy to fulfill the things that you have passion for. The body does not need to grow old at the rate it is. The more in harmony you can be in your inner body, the more fulfilling your life is going to be.

Now I want you to witness, inside of this violet flame, you being out in nature and communing with the plants, animals, fungi, and perhaps with the rocks and the crystals. See yourself understanding their messages and the wisdom that they have to share. Make a conscious effort to connect with all living beings. Understand that you are part of them, and they are a part of you. Everything is connected. Everything has consciousness. It just happens to express itself differently.

Now as you're watching this violet flame in front of you, once again look over at Saint Germain smiling at you. He is inviting you to use this violet flame whenever you need to rid yourself of any of the negative feelings and emotions that you have in this human life. You can burn it all away. He's asking you, as you're looking in the flame, as you do this practice, to be one with the flame. I am the violet flame. I am the violet flame. I am the violet flame.

As you're sitting in this chair, looking at the violet flame, the Agarthan who brought you into Inner Earth is now coming and taking your hand and guiding you once more through this community, this environment. Take in any new details that you might notice. Allow yourself to see it, to feel it, to hear it, and to know it. Your Agarthan is giving you a final parting message. Receive it now. Receive the message. Let it come to you.

They ask you to be a steward of your own community. Honor Earth to be in tune with nature, with Mother Gaia, knowing that everything that you do at the surface has a direct ripple effect on the inside of this Earth. It's all connected. You doing your part will play a huge role in uplifting Earth and transitioning to a fifth-dimensional, awakened reality. Know that we have neighbors inside of the Earth that we can connect with. We can commune with. They help balance Mother Gaia from the inside. They are protectors of Mother Gaia and her energy. They are protectors of some of the dragon realm and some of the other elementals, such as the faeries, the elves, and the dwarves.

Now, it's time to go back to the entrance of the tunnel from which you came from. Whether it's the portal, the dragon, the spaceship, or some other means of transportation, go back through the tunnel now, moving through time, space, and dimension through this tunnel. Come out on the other side of the tunnel back to Earth and back to the room with the chairs. As you're back in this room across from the Agarthan or the multiple Agarthans there with you, thank them for taking you on this journey, sharing their messages, giving you the gift, and knowing that you can connect with them any time you choose.

Many of you connect with them in your astral travels, in your dream state. A lot of you are also helping to balance Mother Gaia from the outside perspective. You're working in conjunction with these Inner Earth beings to help balance Mother Gaia. You are an important point of energy wherever you are on this Earth. The more you can hold this higher vibration, this fifth-dimensional *vibration, the more that humanity evolves and awakens as a collective consciousness, shifting into that fifth-dimensional reality, as a collective, shifting into harmony, into community, becoming one with nature. As above, so below. As within, so without. All is connected.*

Journal prompt:

Take a few moments to write down what you experienced.

Write down the feelings that you had and the energy that you received.

What was the experience of being with the Agarthan that was there with you?

What did your Agarthan look like?

What was their message?

What was their name?

What gift did you receive?

What did Inner Earth look like?

How did being a part of the Violet Flame of Saint Germain feel?

How can you be a better steward of your community?

Chapter 4

Andromedans

Who are the Andromedans?

There are two different groups of Andromedans that interact with us here on Earth. One group comes from the Andromeda galaxy. The other group, which is more prevalent, comes from the Andromeda constellation within our Milky Way galaxy. Within the Andromedan constellation are many different races, some of which are human-like. The Andromedan humanoids are descendants of Lyrans, who left the Lyra constellation during the Lyran-Draconian wars.

Some of these beings have the appearance of being blue-skinned and hairless, somewhat similar to the Arcturians. Others could be more likened to the appearance of Nordic, Mediterranean, and Asian humans. Their eyes are a little larger than those of Earth-based humans. They range between seven to ten feet tall, with elongated, thin bodies.

Some Andromedans are etheric-winged beings that have interacted with Earth since life formed. There may be a correlation between these winged beings and the depictions on Sumerian stone reliefs. Some people also speculate that they might be related to the Archangels.

Andromedans have been described as feeling like heavenly stars – true nirvana. They teach unconditional love and counsel different star nations. They are associated with some of the crop circles found around Earth. They focus on peace resolution. Some visit Earth in merkaba-shaped, crystalline-shaped, and diamond/pyramid-shaped craft. Their interest in Earth has been more for research than direct interference, as with other races, such as the Sirians.

During a parallel life regression session, I led one of my clients through a journey to meet her galactic family. The being who came forward for her was an Andromedan. When asked what they wanted her to know about them, they shared that they are all about love and peace. I had her ask what their general belief system is in the universe. They answered, *"The universe is all one. We are all working together on a soul mission."*

The energy and wisdom of the Andromedans include:

Peace

Freedom

Justice

Evolution

Stones/crystals to help you connect:

blue aventurine, amazonite, lapis lazuli, blue calcite, sodalite, and other blue stones (and any other stones that you are called to work with)

Journal prompt:

Are there any places in your life where you feel injustice?

Where do you want more peace in your life?

Where are you stuck and could use more freedom?

What can you release?

What would evolution look like in your life?

Summary of the Andromedan Journey

In this session, the Andromedans guide you to release any injustices in your life. They help you visualize your life in peace. They help you identify things in your life that you can release to feel more freedom.

The induction part of the journey to raise your vibration and activate your DNA has been omitted. Please refer to Chapter 2 for the process to get yourself into a higher vibrational state of mind.

Journey to Meet Your Andromedan

See a door in front of you. Walk towards the door, knowing that on the other side of this door is a room with two chairs. Go ahead and walk through the door now. Sit yourself down in the comfy chair facing another very comfortable chair, knowing you are safe in this room. Only that which is of your highest and greatest good, only that which is of love, will come into your space today. As you sit in this chair, notice a gray mist around the door. That gray mist is getting thicker and thicker. Your Andromedan family, guides, or perhaps even an aspect of yourself is coming through this gray mist. They're moving towards you, and now they're sitting down in the chair. You now have clear vision of who is in front of you in that chair. How many are there with you?

Look at them. Look at their face. Look into their eyes. Get a sense of whether this is your family, if it's a guide, or if it's an aspect of yourself. As you look at them in that other chair, take in the details of what they look like. What color are their eyes? Do they have hair or not? What color is their skin? Are they wearing any clothing? Anything that you can notice the details of, trust yourself to see this. Feel the love that they have for you. Really look into their eyes, this beautiful being in front of you. Take in their love. Take in their beauty.

They came with a message for you today. Receive the message now. It may come through telepathy or images. They may speak it. Receive the message that they have for you now. They have a gift that they brought for you today. Hold your hands out and receive the gift that they brought for you. You may understand what it is. You may not. Just receive the gift. Let that image come clearly to you. Feel it in your hands. You have this connection. Ask them what the purpose of this gift is for you today, in this time and space. Why this gift? Receive that answer now.

Ask them if they have a name that they would like to be called. Some of them will. Some of them won't. The name may be easy for you to understand. It may be more challenging. Receive the name if they want to give you one right now. Thank them for the message, gift, and the name if they gave one to you.

Once again, look into their eyes. Your chairs are close enough that you're able to hold their hands in your hands. Feel their hands. Feel their energy as you hold their hands and look into their eyes. Focus on any place in your life where you felt there might have been injustice. Bring that up into your mind. Share that with your Andromedan. As you do, they're going to help you balance that injustice into one that is fair and right. They're going to help you be able to speak your truth. To help you do this, we're going to use the energy of the blue throat chakra. Allow yourself to release any energy you're still holding on to with any perceived injustices in your life. Allow yourself to be in a neutral place now in your life, balanced.

As you're still sitting there with your Andromedan, holding their hands, pull up the area where you would like more peace in your life. Telepathically show the Andromedan where you could use more peace in your life and allow them to help you transmute that energy now. Feel the peace in your body. See what this would look like, being so at peace in your life, feeling so at peace in your life. Feel it. See it. Allow that to become your truth. No matter what chaos is going on around you, be that calm eye of the hurricane. You get to choose the peace of your environment, of your mind. The outside factors cannot disturb your peace unless you allow them to. As you see this peace in your environment, as you create peace in your direct environment, you inspire others to create peace in their environment. That creates a ripple effect out into Earth's energy field. Now, visualize peace on Earth. See humans in harmony and peace with each other. No more warring. No more famine. No more strife. Know that this is a timeline that exists. The more that you create that peaceful environment in your life, the more that this will become your reality where there is peace on Earth. It's time to stop fighting against yourself. It's time to stop fighting within your family, with friends, with acquaintances, and with strangers. Your energy is better spent creating a peaceful environment for yourself.

As you are feeling this peace within your body, this peace within your mind, I want you to shift your focus to what you can release in your life to give yourself more freedom - freedom to be who you are, freedom to do what you want to do in your life. What would it look like to be free of people, places, things, times, and events? Free of obligations or expectations. You have the ability to choose what you want to put your attention to and where you want your energy to go. See this vision in your mind. What would that look like for you? Show this vision to the Andromedan whose hands you were still holding and allow them to help you transmute that into reality. As you pull up this image, seeing and feeling this freedom, we will help usher that in with the frequency of the crown chakra.

Freedom equals expansion. Expansion equals evolution. What do you see your evolution like? How are you expanding in your life with this newfound freedom and peace? Take yourself down the timeline where you are completely at peace. Injustices have been balanced out. You are free from expectations and obligations. Now, what does your life look like? How does it evolve? As your crown is wide open, you can allow all of the information and energy from Source to come down into your body. It gives you the information that you need. It gives you the energy you need whenever you need to call on it, whenever you want to connect with your Andromedan.

As you sit across from your Andromedan, receive a parting message from them. Allow yourself to take in their wise words now. Thank them for their message. Ask them to show you a sign that they are there with you, a definitive sign that you will understand when you see it. They agreed to this. And so it is. Once again, look into the eyes of your Andromedan. Feel your body merge with theirs. Feel their energy, the high vibration of what they feel like, so you know it is them when they are around you. Merge into one, where you are looking out of their eyes. Their eyes are your eyes. Feel the energy of how expanded they are, how free they are. They are not bound by any limitations or restrictions. They are able to speak their truth and able to remain in a peaceful environment. They are an inspiration to others. They create peace in their own lives, staying out of the arguing and becoming more of an observer. Now, once again, returning to your own chair, splitting apart, thank them for being here with you today in this time and space.

Journal prompt:

Take a few moments to write down what you experienced.

Write down the feelings that you had and the energy that you received.

What was the experience of being with the Andromedan that was there with you?

What did your Andromedan look like?

What was their message?

What was their name?

What gift did you receive?

What does your evolution look like?

How did it feel to have your body merge with theirs?

What injustices were you able to release?

How did it feel to be in so much peace?

Chapter 5

Arcturians

Who are the Arcturians?

Arcturians originate from the star of Arcturus in the Bootes constellation. They reside in higher dimensional, non-physical form. However, they can lower their vibration to interact with Earth humans as an inward journey. In their physical appearance, they have large heads with large dark eyes. Their bodies are thin, with blueish skin and no hair. Their skin has an amphibian-like quality to it. They emit an energy of pure love.

The Arcturians primarily exist in sixth density and have been attributed to the angelic kingdom. Their energy is also perceived as Christ or Buddha frequency. They manifest to Earth humans according to the beliefs of the person experiencing them. For instance, if a person is religious or believes in angels, they will appear as angels. For others, like me, they appear more as extraterrestrials. For others, they can show up as our future selves. All of this is correct. No matter how the manifestation shows up, they embody love. They are felt as an energy of unconditional love and a surge of creativity.

Arcturus is a higher-dimensional reality which acts as a dimensional gateway to Earth. All those who incarnate on Earth pass through the Arcturian realm before reaching the planet, which provides healing to those born. There are some who consciously choose not to move through the Arcturus gateway. Likewise, at death, human consciousness passes through the Arcturian realm. It is the perceived light at the end of the tunnel and in near-death experiences.

Arcturians are here to be of service to denser realities, such as Earth. They aid in the consciousness from many levels of awareness. In addition to Earth, they serve physicality and interact with other worlds whose evolution is different from humanoids, including plants, minerals, and animals. Their primary service for physical beings is that of emotional healing.

Arcturians have no karmic debt, so rather than incarnating on Earth into a physical body through birth, they "walk-in" to an existing body instead. If there is a soul of a human who is in emotional pain, the human soul will enter the Arcturus realm for healing, and the Arcturian will temporarily inhabit the Earth body. The

Arcturus vibration heals, nurtures, and rejuvenates the human spirit.

The Arcturian energy is infused with creativity. When one is creating, one's energy aligns with the Creator. It is the vibration of creation, healing, and evolution. The reminder to humanity of the unseen connection to Source and the Arcturian emotional healing energy is triggered by the presence of lenticular clouds. They are associated with some of the crop circles on Earth as well.

Arcturians interacted with the early culture of Lemuria by teaching healing skills. Due to their higher frequency, they were not experienced as physical beings, so the information was transmitted through meditation and similar practices. This was before the Pleiadian influence of that civilization. When other extraterrestrial groups started infiltrating Lemuria, the Earth-based Arcturians went underground to become caretakers of the planet's energy. Although the statues of Easter Island are thought to be connected to the Pleiadians, Germane (the multidimensional being who Lyssa Royal-Holt channels) says they actually pay tribute to Arcturian teachers of Lemuria.

As I shared in the first chapter, the Arcturians were the first group I connected with spiritually. They have been guiding me through this process of channeling their messages. They were also the bridge for me to connect with these other galactic races we are exploring in this book. The healing energy I use in my work with clients comes directly from the Arcturian realm. As Arcturian Uluru, I am a healer. Arcturians themselves do not have illness or disease, as those do not exist in the higher dimensions. I channel the healing energy down to me as Earth Lisa through the clear quartz crystal they gave to me in the initial remembering of them during the psychic/intuition class. Using their energy, I help clear away stuck energy created through unprocessed emotions in the human body. Trapped emotions manifest as physical illness and disease, so when we can clear the emotion, the body is able to heal itself.

The energy and wisdom of the Arcturians includes:

Emotional Healing

Love

Unity

Creativity

Stones/crystals to help you connect:

amazonite, sodalite, blue calcite, lapis lazuli, larimar, turquoise, and other stones in the blue and teal family;

rose quartz (and any other stones that you are called to work with)

Journal prompt:

Where in your life are you holding onto trauma, shame, guilt, anger, or other emotions that are not of love and joy?

What emotions are you ready to release?

Who are the people involved in the stuck emotions?

Summary of the Arcturian Journey

In this session, the Arcturians guide you to release any emotions stuck in your body by running white Source light energy through your body. They share a beautiful message of love and unity and follow your passion.

The induction part of the journey to raise your vibration and activate your DNA has been omitted. Please refer to Chapter 2 for the process to get yourself into a higher vibrational state of mind.

Journey to Meet Your Arcturian

Imagine there is a door in front of you. Walk over to the door. On the other side of the door is a cozy room with two comfy chairs. Go ahead and move through the door. Take a seat in one of the two chairs that are facing each other. As you're sitting there in this very comfortable chair, moving through the door now is one of your Arcturian guides. They are sitting down in front of you in the other comfy chair. Greet them in your mind and allow them to greet you.

Stare into their eyes. Really picture their face. Look at their face and look into their eyes. Feel the high vibrational energy that they bring into this space. Feel the love that they have for you, pure love energy. As you're sitting there looking across from them, really connect. Hold your hands out and let them touch your hands. Let that energy pass between you, physically sharing energy between the hands and still staring into the eyes. Allow all of their energy to move through you – their energy of love, their energy of creativity, their energy to heal whatever emotions still need to be healed. Feel the energy exchange.

While you're looking into their eyes, receive a message from them right now, your own personal message from your specific Arcturian guide that's in front of you. It may come through telepathy. You may hear it in your head. It may come as images or symbols. Allow that message to come to you now.

Ask them if they have a name they would like to be called. Some of them will. Some of them may not. Go ahead and receive a name if they have one to give to you. It may be something very familiar to you. It may be something you can't pronounce. Don't judge it. Just let it come.

They brought a gift for you today. While you're still holding your hands out, allow them to present you with a gift. It may be something that you recognize. You may not understand what it is. Receive the gift. Ask what the purpose of this specific gift is for you. Receive that answer from them. Thank them for the gift. As you sit there still looking into their eyes, really see who they are. Feel that energy. Perhaps this is one of your guides. Perhaps it's one of your family members, or perhaps it's another version of yourself.

As you're sitting there looking into their eyes, scan the timeline of your life, this Earth life. Bring into your mind all of the emotions you are still holding on to that might be holding you back. It could be trauma, shame, guilt, anger, or something else that is not serving you. Bring up those feelings, those emotions, to the surface of your mind. Imagine white light energy coming in through your body, running down through your body, and out through the bottom of your feet. Imagine all of these emotions flowing out through the bottom of your feet into the center of the Earth to be recycled, cleansing you and clearing away the debris. Run the white light energy. Imagine wherever that emotion is trapped in the body. The white light is breaking it apart into tiny particles. Allow it to dissolve into the white light energy and to flow out through the bottom of your feet into the center of the Earth. You may have the emotions stuck in different spots in the body. You may feel sensations as it's being released. If you're feeling any tension, put your focus on that area of your body to allow that white light to break apart the mass of energy that is stuck. Allow it to be released, no longer holding on to the energy keeping you stuck in your life.

Think about the people who were involved in creating these emotions that no longer serve you. Understand that you learned lessons from these experiences. There is no right or wrong in it. It's time to understand why these things may have happened for your growth and evolution. Understand what was going on in your life that you needed to learn. Release any shame or guilt that you might be feeling. Release any anger or hatred towards someone you perceive did you wrong, any trauma that has been held in your body. Just keep running that white light through your body, seeing it all clear away. It's safe to let it go. It no longer serves you. It's time to let the past go. It's time to focus on the now. In the now, you are perfectly healed. Keep running the white light through your body.

We are the Arcturians. We come in love and peace. We are so very happy to have you here today in this session with us, with this channel, Lisa, with our energy, with your guide, your family, and perhaps even your own expression of yourselves. Today, we bring to you the energy of love. We want you to feel how much we love you. No matter what has ever happened in this life or any other life, we always love you. We are one with each other.

We want you to imagine that each person in this session is connected to each other. They are all united by this energy that we are bringing. Now, we want you to imagine that energy extending out into the rest of the Earth. You are connected to all humans. We want you now to expand that out into the Universe. You are connected to every living being in your galaxy, your universe, and the multiverses beyond this universe. You are connected to everything. It is all energy. You are all connected to Source. From that Source, you are just simply living an individual expression, but you are not really separate. You need to understand this from our perspective. The more that you understand that you and the person next to you and the person on the other side of the Earth are connected, that you are one, the more love, the more understanding that you can have in your life and for the people in your direct community and your direct relationships.

That love, that unity, that understanding helps heal your beautiful Mother Gaia. She is in much pain. She needs your help in elevating the vibration, elevating the frequency, and living in as much of a state of love as you can. Understand that we are all connected. You are me. I am you. We are one and the same. That is how we can love you so very much.

Some of you are still holding on to some emotions that may not have been quite released. Just know that this will continue to release itself from you. How this happens is that you stay in the present. You do not go back to the past. You do not bring up old memories that are living in the past. Allow yourself to focus on a perfect healthy body and a perfect healthy emotional state. Put yourself into a place of love and joy as often as you can. From that place of love and joy, you will then create a beautiful life in all areas.

It's time to let go of the old stories and baggage you are holding on to. The only person that it is hurting is you. Because you are one of everything, one of everyone, it does have a ripple effect out into those in your world. This deep inner healing ultimately has a ripple effect out into the solar system, the universe, and the multiverses. Your direct healing of yourself matters. It will change the dynamics in your relationships. It will change the dynamics in your job, in your business, and in your *financial life. It is okay to have this sense of peace and joy.*

We want you to follow your passion. That is where we love this creative energy that we can help usher in for you. Where in your life could you use more passion? Follow that passion, and you will not go wrong. When you are in a state of joy, love, and passion, that is how you create a beautiful reality for yourself, no matter what is happening in the world around you. That allows you to keep a healthy emotional state. Yes, there are going to be moments. Of course, you are human and have emotions that come and go. We want to share with you that it is not okay to have those emotions stuck and trapped in your body unless you choose to keep them there because they serve you for a purpose.

We ask that you connect with your Arcturian that you met in this room each day, whether it's in the morning, in the afternoon, or before you go to bed. We ask that you invite them into your space, into your world, and ask them to continue providing this healing energy for the emotions. You have free will. They want to connect, but they need to be invited. Invite them now that you know them. You know who they are. You know their energy. You know they love you so very much. They want to help you. They want to be there to guide you, to support you. Some of you will also start channeling them, just as this channel Lisa does for me. Some of you, the Arcturian that came to you, is you, in a different dimension, a different life. At the quantum level, all lifetimes exist simultaneously. Even though we could call this a past life or a future life, it is actually a parallel life. You are multidimensional, just like we are. We can exist in multiple expressions. That might help some of you feel more comfortable connecting, knowing it is simply another aspect of who you are. We love you so very much. Thank you for letting us connect with you today.

Journal prompt:

Take a few moments to write down what you experienced.

Write down the feelings that you had and the energy that you received.

What was the experience of being with the Arcturian that was there with you?

What did your Arcturian look like?

What was their message?

What was their name?

What gift did you receive?

Recognize if there are any additional places in your body where you are feeling there is stuck energy.

Allow yourself to release the emotions trapped in your body.

Chapter 6

Blue Avians

Who are the Blue Avians?

The Blue Avians come from the Lyra constellation, where the human form originated in our galaxy. They are an avian-mammalian form that appears bipedal with a bird-like head and blue feathers covering the body. They believe in "service to others" and are here to help Earth understand Unity Consciousness. They reside in a much higher dimensional reality, mostly in the twelfth dimension.

Avian humanoid extraterrestrials have a long history of interacting with humanity worldwide. They are known as bird gods in native cultures. Ancient Sumeria has a bird god called Ninurta. Australia has a bird god called Bunjil. In Egypt, they include Horus, Ra, and Thoth. The Aztec culture has Huitzilopochtli, also known as Totec. Garuda is the Hindu bird god. In Native American culture, the thunderbird is the powerful bird god.

As a race, Blue Avians are not as interactive with humans on Earth compared to the other galactic races we are exploring in this book, so not as much is known about them. During the galactic sessions I led in the first part of 2023, they were the last group I channeled due to their very high vibration. They were only offered as a bonus group for those who had signed up for the entire galactic experience because it was important that those experiencing them had gone through all of the other processes of the other groups first. One must be in the highest vibrational state possible to connect with them.

The energy and wisdom of the Blue Avians include:

Consciousness

Expansion

Nurture

Vibration

Stones/crystals to help you connect:

amethyst, lepidolite, lapis lazuli, larimar, amazonite, sodalite, blue calcite, turquoise, and other stones in the purple, blue, and teal family (and any other stones that you are called to work with)

Journal prompt:

How can you nurture yourself more?

In your day-to-day life, where do you typically vibrate – low, medium, or high?

What would it take for you to expand your consciousness?

Summary of the Blue Avian Journey

In this session, the Blue Avians help you to create a Merkaba around your body so that when the pyramids spin opposite each other, it creates a zero-point energy field. In this high vibrational state, they take you on a journey to the void, allowing you to fully reset yourself to a neutral state.

The induction part of the journey to raise your vibration and activate your DNA has been omitted. Please refer to Chapter 2 for the process to get yourself into a higher vibrational state of mind.

Journey to Meet Your Blue Avian

In front of you, see a door. On the other side of that door is a room with two comfy chairs. Go ahead and move through the door and sit down in one of these two chairs that are facing each other. Look over at the door. See a gray mist starting to form around the door. The gray mist is getting thicker and thicker, twirling now around the door, allowing your Blue Avian to come through the door. There may be one or more Blue Avians with you in the room. One of them is now sitting in the chair directly across from you.

Look at them. See them clearly. Look at the details. Starting with their head, what does their head look like? What shape is it? Do they look more humanoid, or do they look more bird-like? Do they have feathers on their face and their head or not? What color are these feathers, if they have them, or their skin? What color do you see? Take a look at their eyes. What shape and size are their eyes? What do they look like? What color are their eyes? Just let it come to you. Take a look at their nose and their mouth. Do they have any sort of beak feature, or do they look more humanoid or something else? There is no right or wrong in this. Just let it come. Do they have any kind of external ears that you can see?

Now, look down at their body. Are they wearing any clothing or not? If they're wearing clothing, what does this look like? What color is their clothing? If they're not wearing clothing, what do their bodies look like? Do they look like human bodies? Do they have feathers or something else? Now they're holding up their hands. Take a look at their hands if you can see them. Do you notice anything interesting about their hands? Do they have fingers like we do or something else? If they do have fingers, how many do they have? Now, look down at their feet. Do they have any kind of shoe covering on, or are they barefoot? If they're barefoot, what do their feet look like? Take in these details.

Looking into the eyes of this Blue Avian, get a sense of this Blue Avian. Are they part of your galactic family? Are they one of your guides, or are they an aspect of you? Let that answer come now. They came with a message for you today in this room. I want you to receive their message. It may come through the words that they speak. It may be through telepathy or images. Allow their message to come to you now.

They brought a gift for you. Hold your hands out and receive their gift. See it clearly. Feel it in your hands. Ask them what this gift means for you in this space right now. Let that answer come to you.

Ask them if they have a name that they would like to be called. Some of them will. Some of them won't. Some names are easy. Others are not as easy to understand or pronounce. Let their name come to you if they have one to give you. Thank them for their message, for the gift, and their name if they gave you one.

Look deeply into their eyes. Feel the wisdom that they have. Feel their energy in your body. Allow what they *know to flow into you, into your mind, as telepathic messages. You may understand their language of what they are sending to you. It may be images. It may be something that's completely foreign. Just simply receive what it is they are sending to your mind now. They have codes they are giving you to activate even more of your DNA. Those of you in the presence of their energy are ready to shift into higher consciousness. You are ready to expand.*

Now, in your hands, they are giving you an image of a Merkaba, turning into a physical Merkaba, a double tetrahedron. It's getting bigger and bigger. This double tetrahedron Merkaba is now surrounding your body. Feel the energy of these two pyramids opposite each other, surrounding your body. Now, I want you to see the top one spinning clockwise around your body. The one pointing downwards is now spinning counterclockwise around your body, creating a shield, an energy field around your body. See these pyramids spinning faster and faster, opposite each other. They are spinning so fast that they are becoming spherical. You're creating a bubble energy shield around your body, a safe atmosphere for which to travel. Your vibration is so high now in this bubble, this double tetrahedron. It's spinning and twisting around you, counterclockwise, clockwise, rotating against each other, creating a zero-point energy field. Feel your body now, so light in this bubble sphere.

See and feel your body rising up above the ground. You are so light. You can will this to happen. You are simply energy. See yourself raising, levitating above the ground, knowing that you are safe as you do this. Put your thoughts on traveling to the void, the darkness of the void. As you put your thoughts there, as you are spinning in this bubble, you are instantly transported to the void. As you're within this safe bubble, feel what this void feels like. See what it looks like, this darkness all around you, the point of creation. This is where you come from. This is who you really are. There is nothing to be afraid of, the darkness. It is the point of all creation. Feel so completely at home in this dark space, this void. This is the ultimate place of neutrality. All potentials exist in this point.

Now, just experience yourself being in this void and let the frequency expand your consciousness. Even more potentials exist in this place. What potential do you want to create? This is ground zero right here. From this place of being in the void, expand your consciousness out to see the sparkling quantum energy move down through the dimensions to physically incarnate here on Earth. See yourself being the creator, the true creator. What is it that you want to create? Allow yourself to expand beyond what you have ever dreamed of.

You're still inside of this bubble, inside of the void. Allow yourself to feel so at peace, so at ease, in this void, completely resetting your emotional structure and environment. Create a new reality for yourself within this bubble, within this void. The more you can return to this void, the easier it will be to shift things in your life. In this void space, it is the pause. It is the resting point. This is truly how you can nurture yourself in this Earth human life. Feel how light and free you are in this bubble, within the void, your own energy field that nothing can penetrate. You are so completely safe here within this field. This resides within you. You create this energy field simply by visualizing it, knowing it, and speaking it into existence. There is no time in this place. All things exist simultaneously within this void.

In order to get to this space, there is a practice of shifting into a very high vibrational state of being. Release all the thoughts of your monkey mind, to just be one, to be present within this void where nothing exists, and all things exist. Within this bubble, once again, see this spinning of your energy field. You have two fields spinning opposite each other to create the zero-point energy. Bring it up in your mind. See the spinning clockwise and counterclockwise. Feel this vibration of what it's generating in your body. You might even sense the sound of this vibration, the reverberating kind of sound, perhaps like helicopter or fan blades spinning, or perhaps some other kind of sound. Tune in. Open your mind to your clairaudience and hear this vibration.

Within your energy field, just with the thought of your mind, go to your most favorite place that you can imagine. This sphere will instantly take you there. See yourself just with the thought within this energy field. Now you're fully surrounded in your favorite place that you can imagine, surrounded by the things you love. You can take yourself to this place whenever you choose. You can travel there within your bands, within your energy field.

In your bubble, in your field, take yourself back to the room with the chairs and sit in your chair again. Your pyramids are starting to slow down. You're coming back into a more present reality within this room, with your Blue Avian in front of you. Once again, look into their eyes. Receive their final message that they have for you today. Receive it now.

You have so much potential. You are invited to raise your vibration regularly to connect with us and all of the higher dimensional beings that you have. When you do this, it expands your consciousness beyond your comfort zone, opening you up to new possibilities. That allows you to know your full power of who you are and who you came to be. You are so much more than this one human life. You are multidimensional, just like all the groups you have worked with. You have the ability to raise your vibration to experience the higher dimensional realms. The more you raise your consciousness, the more that expands all possibilities for you in all timelines.

Do not limit yourself. Do not be afraid. Understand that there is absolutely nothing to fear because everything is connected within that void space you just visited. You are connected to everything, everyone. From that place, you create your reality. That is the place where you truly nurture the essence of who you are. It is remembering who you are. Nurturing at an Earth level is very different from nurturing your soul and your light. The void is the true reset of the body, physical and emotional, of the mind.

Just know how great you are. You are one of everything. You are not lesser than any of us who reside in these higher dimensions. You are equals. You are just choosing a different experience at this moment. You are helping to expand the experiences within this universe and the multiverses that exist beyond this universe.

Once again, thank your Blue Avian for being in this time and place, with you knowing that you can connect with them whenever you choose. When you raise your frequency up as high as you did today to connect with them, it affects every cell of your body. It expands you beyond what you could ever hope to know in this Earth life in such beautiful ways.

Journal prompt:

Take a few moments to write down what you experienced.

Write down the feelings that you had and the energy that you received.

What was the experience of being with the Blue Avian that was there with you?

What did your Blue Avian look like?

What was their message?

What was their name?

What gift did you receive?

What did it feel like to spin your Merkaba around your body?

How did it feel to be in the void?

Chapter 7

Hybrids

Who are the Hybrids?

Hybrids, as defined here, are a spiritually advanced race of beings that have been created by combining Zeta and Earth human DNA. This is a soul contract between the Zeta and human before the human is born on Earth. Generally, the humans involved in the hybridization program have lived a Zeta life and chose the human experience to be a part of this formation of a spiritually advanced race of beings. Most people forget they volunteered to help and agreed to the contract, so fear sometimes happens during the experience.

There are two major groups of Hybrids with subcategories of each. One group is the Essassani, half Zeta and half Earth human living on ships. They may be the first to integrate with us by living here on Earth. The other group is the Yahyel, which are Zetas and Earth humans who are very human-like.

Long ago, Zetas modified their genetics to breed out emotions in their race because they believed emotions got in the way of their evolution. They thought the logical mind was supreme. They didn't realize that no longer having emotions would make them sterile. After realizing their mistake, they chose Earth-based humans as a perfect race to co-create an advanced race. The hybrid program combines the best parts of the Zeta DNA with the best features of the Earth human DNA, including some of the human emotions.

Humans are temporarily detained or taken by the Zetas onto their spacecraft. Often those detained report their eggs and sperm have been taken from them. Some women know they are pregnant and get confirmation from the doctor, but then the baby is removed from the womb early in development. The doctors are unable to explain why. Some men and women have experienced being able to see their hybrid children. In their dream state, human mothers (and some fathers) are taken aboard the ships where their Hybrid children live so that they can give them the love and affection that the Zetas cannot provide.

In 2023, I received confirmation that I am part of this Zeta-Human Hybrid program. I know I would have enthusiastically volunteered for this. I have several friends who consciously know they are part of the program as well. Some of them remember meeting their Hybrid children.

The energy and wisdom of the Hybrids include:

Choice

Clarity

Manifestation

Release

Stones/crystals to help you connect:

dragon blood stone, unakite, green calcite, orange calcite, and other stones in the orange and green family (and any other stones that you are called to work with)

Journal prompt:

What do you want to manifest in your life?

Where do you need to grow or evolve to make it happen?

Where do you need more balance?

Summary of the Hybrid Journey

In this session, the Hybrids take you on a journey in a spacecraft to the quantum realm. In this place, seeing the blue grid that connects all things, they guide you through manifesting thought into physical form. They help you to balance your life and release what no longer serves you. They help you identify what parts of your environment might need to change to help you manifest your desires more easily.

The induction part of the journey to raise your vibration and activate your DNA has been omitted. Please refer to Chapter 2 for the process to get yourself into a higher vibrational state of mind.

Journey to Meet Your Hybrid

As you're sitting across from one or more Hybrids, ask this Hybrid sitting in the chair in front of you if you are part of the Hybrid program in one form or another, and simply get a yes or a no. And if you get a yes, I want you to ask if you are part of the Zeta side. Yes or no? Are you part of the human side? Yes or no? Are you one of the Hybrids that is being created? Yes or no? You might have gotten a yes for all three or just one or two of them. There is no right or wrong with this. Trust the answers that come to you.

Look deeply into their eyes. Feel their energy. Feel and know the wisdom they have to bring to you today. See your body now merging with theirs. Hold their hands and allow your energy to merge together. See through the eyes of the Hybrid that you were sitting in front of. Your perspective may be completely different out of these new eyes that you're looking through. I want you, inside of their energy, inside of their body, to know the wisdom that they have, the connection that they have with you.

You're now going to take a journey as this Hybrid. There is a spaceship outside of the door. Get up out of the chair as this Hybrid and walk over to where the spaceship is. Now you're going to get inside of the spaceship, sitting down in a very comfy chair. Put your hands on the console, letting your hands fuse with the craft so it can read your mind to take you where you are ready to go. The craft is now taking off, and you're moving through time, space, and dimension. As you're moving through space, very clearly see the darkness, the void, the empty space, and the perceived empty space between the stars.

Now, in this blackness, see a blue grid connecting all of the stars, the pinpoints, together. Ultraviolet blue light connects every point of light you see, creating this blue gridline field of reality. See how all things are connected to each other in this higher dimensional quantum realm *with the blue grid lines. This is the realm of manifestation.*

As an observer in your spacecraft, seeing these blue grid lines, pull up in your mind what you wrote down earlier of what you want to create in your life. Pull it up in your thoughts. In this Hybrid mind, you are a higher dimensional being where instant manifestation occurs in this fifth-dimensional realm. The thought is there, and as you are looking out over this blue grid field, you see golden-white sparkles starting to form over the blue grid. The energy is densifying into reality, this creation, this thought. See it manifesting right in front of you. See it become densified, physical, in front of you. Above this blue grid, still out in space, see them become a reality from the quantum realm when you shift into this higher dimensional reality, this fifth dimension and higher. Experience from this Hybrid mind, instant manifestation. Allow the energy of the throat chakra, the center for manifestation, to solidify this in every cell of your being, knowing that manifestation is possible. It is reality. You just simply need to shift into this higher dimension. Allow yourself to see this creation and feel the emotions and joy of having created this thing, this thought. See it densify into reality.

Still above the blue grid, out in space, in the quantum realm, still in the body and the mind of the Hybrid, now pull up a new creation, a new thought, perhaps some-

thing completely different than what you just created. Bring up a new creation of what you want to manifest.

Once again, see it coalescing, becoming a reality in front of you. Above this blue grid, sparkles come together, the energy coming together to create the form, to densify the form into reality. With the sound, with the voice, your throat chakra, speak it into manifestation. Speak it into form.

Now, once again, over the blue grid, in a different location, pull a new thought into your mind, a new creation. As you visualize this creation, I want you to also speak it into reality, using your voice, using the throat, in addition to the thought. See that come together, densifying, becoming physical reality. Allow yourself to know without a doubt that you have the ability to manifest your reality, to create your reality. It is as simple as raising your vibration, being so clear in your thought, so clear in the words that you are speaking, that it manifests instantly in front of you in this higher realm.

Experience the joy that goes with this manifestation. Feel that evolved emotion, that evolved state of being in your body, as you know you can create anything you desire in this dimension. It's going into every cell of your body, helping your third and fourth-dimensional human body to remember this experience of creation, of manifestation. Know that you can do this even in this third-density reality. It takes a little more time to *densify into form, but when you shift yourself into the higher dimensional quantum realm and create it there, it will percolate down into this Earth human experience that you are simultaneously living.*

Now, still in this Hybrid body, looking at this blue grid in front of you, imagine your Earth human body in front of you. See yourself as your Earth-human self, looking through the eyes of the Hybrid. I want you with full knowingness to understand what you need to change or where you need to grow and evolve as an Earth human to make this reality of instant manifestation true for you. Where could you evolve? Is this a new practice? Is it a new belief system? Perhaps it's just taking the steps. Observe yourself making those changes, evolving in front of your very eyes, shifting into the human who understands that you create your reality.

You have total control over that creation. You are in control of the thoughts going on in your mind. You understand that if there aren't any thoughts that go against what you are trying to create, and you can grow and evolve and correct those, to be so fully in line with what you desire to manifest, it has no other choice but to become reality. It's when your subconscious thoughts fight against your conscious thoughts that stunts your ability to create. As you Earth humans are shifting into a higher dimensional existence, as you're moving towards fifth-dimensional reality and you maintain those states of joy and passion, the faster you are going to see your manifestations become reality. You will see them create so much faster than you have ever experienced.

Now, still observing your human self in front of you, understand where you, as Earth human are out of balance in your life. Where are you out of balance in your emotions? Where are you too wrapped up that you are getting in your own way? See this without judgment of yourself. Just notice what it is. Now, see your Earth human self getting yourself back into balance. That may be different aspects of your life. It may be your emotions. Feel in this Hybrid body what it feels like to be fully in balance, in balance again of the emotions, not letting them rule your world, experiencing them and letting them flow through you. You are not holding on. You are not becoming addicted to those emotions. Allow yourself to be in a higher state of joy, passion, and love. Observe it as your Earth human that's in front of you.

See the shifts that being in balance makes in your body. Perhaps your anatomy changes. Perhaps your physiology changes. The inside thoughts are creating your outside physical reality of your body, your environment, and everything in your world. The people, places, things, times, and events that are happening in your world are a manifestation of your internal world. See how putting everything into balance shifts that reality. See this from the eyes of the Hybrid, the changes that are being made *in you as Earth human. What feelings, what emotions do you experience seeing this transformation, this evolution, this growth? Feel it in every cell of your body what the balance feels like. Feel the flow with the Universe, the ease and grace you have in your life. Things like pain and suffering are gone.*

Observe your Earth human self going through the process of raising your vibration, shifting into at least a fifth-dimensional reality, seeing the blue grid, and manifesting your thoughts from that place. See them coalesce down here in third-density Earth human reality like shimmering stardust coming down in front of you and creating the physical form of whatever you want to manifest. See your Earth human doing this consciously. The more you consciously create your reality, the better your Earth reality gets, although there is no good or bad. You will experience more joy and more flow.

Notice that you always have a choice in what you are creating. So now again, from the Hybrid eye perspective, see your Earth human experience. See what you want to create in terms of your overall environment here on Earth. Who are the people that you want to have in your life? What are their qualities? There may be specific people that you see, but we also invite you to be open and just focus on the qualities, not on what they look like or that it has to be a certain person. What are the things you want in your life? You are allowed to enjoy being human. That's part of what you came here to do: play the game in whatever way you choose.

What kinds of things would you like to have in your Earth human reality? See it as if it is so because there are realities where it already exists. What kind of environment are you living in? What kind of house? What kind of neighborhood, if you're in a neighborhood? Perhaps you're out in the middle of nowhere. See the environment that fuels your soul, that brings you passion. See yourself in that environment. What kinds of things are you doing in this creation? Are there specific activities you enjoy doing? And if so, see yourself doing these and how much joy it brings into your life, following your passions. If one passion has completed itself, allow yourself to move to a new passion. Allow yourself to explore, to evolve, to grow, to gain the wisdom, and to move on. That is what you are here to experience.

In observing from this Hybrid point of view, understand the connection you have to all things, to all people. All things throughout the universe are connected. You are connected directly to Source. See that connection through those chakras all the way out to the silver chakra directly connected to Source. Know when you connect in those higher dimensional realities, you are able to pull those thoughts down through the chakras into manifestation. You can heal your body with this energy. You can create whatever reality it is that you want, being in balance with your emotions, being in balance in your life. Allow yourself to move through situations, to evolve, and to grow.

Through these Hybrid eyes, fully feel the connection that you have to one another, to every human on Earth, to Mother Gaia, to all of nature, every species whether plant, animal, bacteria, fungi or anything else. Feel the connection, the oneness. Feel the love. Have a beautiful love for all things without judgment.

See yourself back in the spacecraft as the Hybrid flying back towards Earth. As you near Earth, see her beauty. Zoom in to yourself, wherever you are on Earth at this moment. Zoom into yourself having this experience, observing yourself, knowing that every cell of your body has been programmed to understand how to manifest reality. Commit to yourself that you will become more consciously aware of what your thoughts are and what words you are speaking into manifestation. Words and thoughts have full power over your reality.

Zoom in and observe yourself, sending love to yourself. If there are any feelings of guilt, shame, anger, or frustration that you have been holding on to, anything where you are stuck in your emotions as you observe yourself, send love to yourself. Forgive yourself and release those emotions now. Let them melt away. You get to choose whether you hold on to them or not. You're being invited now to release them. It is safe to do that, and it will allow faster evolution and growth, faster manifestation.

Love yourself. See your worth. The more love you have for yourself, the more you can share that love with others. The more you can be vulnerable with yourself, to release those emotions, to forgive yourself, the more you're able to extend that to others. This is what helps shift humanity into a higher conscious reality, to shift into the fifth-dimensional reality where the Hybrids reside. One day, know we will all be united. We will all be able to live with each other without judgment of what anyone looks like or what anyone is doing, just observing without judgment.

Pull yourself out of the Hybrid and back into your human experience. Once again, in the room sitting across from your Hybrid in the chairs, receive a parting message from the Hybrid or Hybrids that came to be with you today to give you this experience. Go ahead and receive the message now.

Journal prompt:

Take a few moments to write down what you experienced.

Write down the feelings you had and the energy you received.

What was the experience of being with the Hybrid who was there with you?

What did your Hybrid look like?

What message did you receive from the Hybrid?

How did it feel to see your thoughts manifesting into physical form in the blue grid?

Chapter 8

Lyrans

Who are the Lyrans?

L yrans originate in the Lyra constellation and come in a variety of forms. They are the original humanoid prototype which all other humanoid races evolved from in our galaxy. The humanoids originally ranged in skin tone from blue, brown, white, yellow, and red. As they evolved over time, their hair, skin, and eyes got lighter. Some humanoid Lyran groups have incorporated other animal DNA into the human form, including primates, reptilians, avians, and felines. Lyrans evolved and achieved space travel, which allowed them to explore and colonize other regions of the galaxy. They can be found in many star systems throughout the galaxy. The Lyran group we are working with in this chapter are the feline humanoids. Some appear more cat-like, including lions, tigers, and domestic cats, with others being more human-like with subtle cat-like features. They are bipedal and may or may not have a tail.

Feline humanoids and cats have played a considerable role in many ancient cultures around Earth. The Ancient Egyptians had numerous feline-humanoid gods and goddesses, including Bastet, Sekhmet, Mut, Tefnut, Shesemtet, Pakhet, Mafdet, and Wadjet. Other feline-like and feline-associated deities include the Mayan Jaguar God of the Underworld, Baron Ket of Indonesia, Lamassu of Assyria, Ai- Apaec of the Mochica civilization, Li Shou of China, Ovinnik of Poland, Hecate of Greece, and Freyja of Norse.

During a parallel life regression session, my client had an unexpected life as a feline humanoid living in the Spica star system. In part of the session, she explained what she looked like and what the community was like.

The message below is part of the transcription from this session:

Client: I can see myself as a cat. Not like how cats walk here, but like cat features.

Lisa: Okay, so like a feline humanoid?

Client: Yes. Yes, and I'm standing on a platform. I'm just standing.

Lisa: Are you male or female?

Client: I'm female, for sure.

Lisa: Can you describe in more detail what your features look like and what color you are?

Client: I am, no, it's not an orange tabby, but like a brown, brownish. I just feel beautiful.

Lisa: Do you like being in this cat?

Client: I think so. It's ideal. I look ideal to their standard.

Lisa: What is your role there?

Client: I feel like I'm powerful, a lot like somebody high up, maybe. But everybody is nice to each other. They all know me.

Lisa: So it's a caring community?

Client: Yes.

Lisa: Are all the others similar in form to you, or are there different types?

Client: They're similar, but I am at the most beautiful. I know it. I have a lot of self-love, but I am nice.

Lisa: Do you wear any clothes?

Client: I can sense jewelry and gold-like clasps in my ears. I have like long, almost like dreadlocks, but I am decorated, I guess.

The energy and wisdom of the Lyrans include:

Adventure

Fearless

Independent

Self-worth

Stones/crystals to help you connect:

red jasper, carnelian, red agate, orange calcite, obsidian, tiger's eye, and other stones in the red, orange, and brown family (and any other stones that you are called to work with)

Journal prompt:

What is a big dream you have?

What are your fears about this dream?

Where do you feel unworthy?

Summary of the Lyran Journey

In this session, the Lyrans merge with you so you can perceive things from their perspective. They help you to move through any fears that are holding you back from achieving your dreams and goals. They guide you to step into the unknown to go on new adventures. They allow you to feel confidence and self-worth as you step forward onto a new timeline towards your desires.

The induction part of the journey to raise your vibration and activate your DNA has been omitted. Please refer to Chapter 2 for the process to get yourself into a higher vibrational state of mind.

Journey to Meet Your Lyran

See a door in front of you right now. Walk towards the door. You're moving in through the door, into the room. Take a seat in one of the two comfy chairs in this room. This chair is sitting across from another chair. As you're sitting in this chair, be very curious about which of the Lyrans is going to come to be with you today to help take you on this journey. Start feeling the presence of one or more of the Lyrans coming through the door. They're now walking towards the chair, and they're sitting down in the chair.

Take a really good look at them. Do they look more cat-like? Do they look more human-like? Get a sense of who they are. Look into their eyes, the windows to the soul. Get a sense of if this is an aspect of you. Or is it one of your family members? Is it one of your guides? You can ask them if you are unsure.

As you're looking into their eyes, they came with a message for you today about who they are, about their relationship to you, and about this journey that you're going to be taking. Receive the message now. This may come as a vision through words or through telepathy. Allow yourself to receive this message from the Lyrans.

Ask them if they have a specific name that they would like to be called. Some of them will, some of them won't. Don't judge the name if they give you one. It may be something you understand immediately. It may be harder to pronounce or not at all. Allow their name to come to you if they want to give you one.

They also brought a gift for you today. Hold your hands out. Receive the gift that they brought for you. You may understand what it is. You may not. Receive the gift. Have clear vision of what this gift is. Ask them what the meaning of this gift is for you today, in this space. What is the purpose or meaning of this gift they are giving to you? Receive that now.

Thank them for their message and the gift, and if they gave you a name for sharing that with you. As you're sitting across from them, look deep into their eyes. Feel the worth they have in themselves, that confidence they have in themselves. They want you to see it in their eyes. They want you to feel it coming off of their body. See how brave they are, how courageous they are, how adventurous they are in stepping into new and unknown territory, how independent they are, not being codependent, and having strong boundaries. See this power within them. Feel the power within them as you look into their eyes.

Hold their hands, with your knees touching, looking into their eyes. See yourself becoming them. See yourself merging with them, putting on this feline-type body, whether it's more humanoid or more cat-like. See your body change. Transform into their body. Feel how strong and powerful it is to be inside of this body that has full self-worth, full confidence, fearless, independent, and adventurous.

Through the eyes of this feline body that you are now within, you're looking out these feline eyes with a new perspective, a different perspective than your own human self. Feel it in your body that you are this being. As you are in this feline body, pull up that image of what your dream was, that goal you wrote down just a little bit ago. See the end of that goal. See what it looks like as if it has already happened. What is going on in this human life with that goal achieved? Who is around you? What are the feelings you have? Is this the goal that you wanted to achieve? Did you get the results? See it. Feel it. This is something that I want to be a really big stretch for the human part of you.

See it through these feline eyes that everything is possible. See that as if it's already been accomplished. It's already been achieved. See that dream, that goal accomplished. I want you to reverse-engineer it. Take a step back from right before you achieved it. What was the situation? What might have been going on in your life, in your mind? Were there still fears and doubts, or did you feel full confidence knowing you were almost there? Take another step back in that timeline. See what might have been going on. Again, were there any doubts, fears, or feelings of worthiness you worked through? You did achieve this goal. You did achieve this dream. What was going on in these previous steps?

Move back to the human part of you, still in this feline body. See yourself from this higher perspective, from this feline perspective, observing the human you. See where you are. See where you doubt yourself. Where do you not feel worthy of achieving this dream? Know that it is okay to have those doubts. It is okay to have those feelings of unworthiness because that is simply a human construct. That is part of the experience. And that is what you are here to transmute today. Pull up those fears, those insecurities, those doubts. Pull them up and allow yourself to release these doubts. Release the unworthiness from your body. Know that you have already achieved this goal. You've already achieved this dream. It's time to release all that so you can move forward easily in this new timeline. All of the fears can be overcome. You can have your fears, and you can move through them.

You are worthy of achieving whatever dreams or goals you may have. Pull in that feline confidence, that feline worthiness. Be excited about the future. Be excited about the unknown possibilities that await you, the adventures that await you in your life. Know that you can achieve whatever you set your mind to do. Know that you can call on this energy, this wisdom of your feline self, to move through these spheres, these doubts, to know your worthiness. Release any codependency you feel, knowing you are strong and independent. You know when to ask for help, which is not codependency. There is a difference in knowing that you are worthy of your dreams and your goals no matter what anyone in your life has told you. You are worthy.

You are allowed to have what you want to have in this Earth life. You just simply need to remember who and what you are and that you have these powers to make your reality come true. You have the ability to manifest your reality. You have the ability to step outside of your comfort zone, which keeps you growing and evolving. When you are not growing or evolving, you are dying. Do you want to keep moving forward and expand in your life? And if so, use this energy. Even if you have fear of the unknown, just take one step into the unknown. This step will appear, and simply take another step and another step. You don't need to know all the steps to get to where you're going. However, they will appear when they are needed when you are ready for those steps.

Now see yourself from this feline perspective as this human, in the place that you are in your life right here, right in this moment. See yourself as a worthy human. Understand that you may have fears that come up. Know that you can step through these fears. All is well. All will be okay as you take the step forward towards your new dream. On the timeline of that new dream, that new goal that you created, you have different choices. Focus on this timeline that you have just created today. Allow whatever feelings that might be coming up about going down that timeline. It may be excitement, anticipation, or uncertainty. Allow whatever emotions are coming up in that. Simply just take one step forward into that timeline. See yourself taking the one step forward that puts you directly in this timeline. Just like you're walking over a very easy bridge, see yourself walking over this bridge. Perhaps it's flat. It might have a little curve to it. You might have to go uphill a little bit and then back down. On the other side of this bridge is that dream, that goal that you wrote down. See yourself walking on this path, on this bridge, step by step, not needing to know what these steps are or what the details are. See yourself taking these steps, moving along the bridge, and getting closer and closer to the other side of that bridge where that dream is reality.

You're already on the timeline. See it happening now. See yourself walking the path, walking the steps. And as you're walking along the bridge, know that you are on this timeline. Feel the emotions in your body of excitement, anticipation, or whatever is coming up as you're walking the bridge. Now, you're coming closer and closer and closer to the end of this bridge. Take the final step from the bridge into this new reality where it's fully manifested. Take the step now. Once again, see how it feels to have achieved this dream. What do you see going on in your life? Who is in your life? What is in your life? Where do you live? What kind of people surround you? What kind of lifestyle do you have?

Take a few moments to fully explore this reality, this dream, and the goal you just manifested. See it. Feel it in your body. As you're exploring it, let the frequency ground that in as your reality, becoming your new reality, your security, your support. Ground yourself into this dream that you just created. Take on the energy of this grounding into this reality. Feel the power and the strength that you have, knowing that you achieved this dream, this goal. You have the power to achieve whatever other dreams and goals that you may have. Feel your strength, your confidence. Know your worthiness. You are worthy to have all that you desire in this life. You have the ability to walk through any fears or doubts that you have. Allow yourself to have an adventurous spirit, a courageous spirit. Know you can step out of your comfort zone into new realities whenever you choose. Allow the solar plexus energy to fill you up with your self-power, your boldness. The only thing that can ever hold you back is yourself. When you're feeling doubts, call in this feline strength, this feline energy.

As you are in this new reality that you've just created, look out into time and space. Imagine the next dream that might want to unfold for you. And as you're in this space, as you're in the feline body, see a spaceship that's landing. Get into the spaceship. See the spaceship. Feel it taking off, out into space where you can see things from a higher perspective. Understand you are unlimited in your potential. You are unlimited in your possibilities. You get to decide where you go next.

What is the next dream? What is the next adventure? Stay curious. Stay open to the possibilities, knowing that all is well. You are always supported. You always have guidance. The only thing holding you back from moving forward is you. Stay in this frequency, this high *vibrational frequency of power, of confidence, of being curious like a cat, being adventurous, fearless, and worthy. Now, see that spacecraft landing wherever you want it to land. Perhaps it's the new dream. Perhaps it's the dream after that dream. Feel once again the energy of this feline body, this feline wisdom, this feline strength. This is who you are. You have this inside of you. Every one of you has this inside of you. It has been activated today. You can call on it whenever you need it.*

Journal prompt:

Take a few moments to write down what you experienced.

Write down the feelings you had and the energy you received.

What was the experience of being with the Lyran that was there with you?

What did your Lyran look like?

What was their message?

What was their name?

What gift did you receive?

What did it feel like to see your dream or goal manifested?

What did it feel like to have the courage and fearlessness of the Lyran?

Are you ready to step into a new timeline of possibility?

What is the first step you can take towards your dream?

Chapter 9

Mantis

Who are the Mantis?

M antis are bipedal beings who look like praying mantis insects. They stand between seven to ten feet tall or more with long limbs. They are highly advanced and evolved and are believed to be among the most ancient groups in the universe. Some of these beings are referred to as The Founders, as they are said to have created the humanoid form in the galaxy.

Although Mantis reside in the fifth-density and higher, they have the ability to lower their vibration to the third and fourth density to have a physical form. They are master geneticists. Some are believed to work with the Zetas on the hybridization program and are commonly seen on the Zeta spacecraft. There are different Mantis races coming from Antares, Andromeda, Orion, and beyond.

The energy and wisdom of the Mantis include:

Ancient Wisdom

Creation

Divine Masculine

Master Healing

Stones/crystals to help you connect:

moss agate, green jade, green calcite, and other green stones (and any other stones that you are called to work with)

Summary of the Mantis Journey

In this session, the Mantis align your 12 chakras within your body and beyond, all the way to Source. They bring forth your original 12-strand DNA to activate all of your powers that are natural to you. They call forth the divine masculine within you and guide you through a manifestation process. Their master healing energy helps to clear anything in the body that needs attention.

The induction part of the journey to raise your vibration and activate your DNA has been omitted. Please refer to Chapter 2 for the process to get yourself into a higher vibrational state of mind.

Journal prompt:

What do you want to create in your life?

Draw a symbol to represent that creation.

What part of you needs healing?

Journey to Meet Your Mantis

We are going to do an alignment of the chakras, adding on chakras 8 through 12. Starting at your root chakra, see red spinning energy, spinning easily and freely. Move up now to your sacral. See the orange spinning energy, spinning in perfect harmony with the red below it. Move up now to your solar plexus. See the yellow spinning energy. The yellow is spinning in perfect harmony with the orange and the red. Move to your heart and see the green spinning energy. The green is spinning in perfect harmony with the yellow, the orange, and the red. Move now to your throat. See the blue spinning energy. The blue is spinning in perfect harmony with the green, the yellow, the orange, and the red. Move to your third eye. See the indigo spinning energy. The indigo is spinning in perfect harmony with the blue, the green, the yellow, the orange, and the red. Move to your crown. See the violet spinning energy. The violet is spinning in perfect harmony with the indigo, the blue, the green, the yellow, the orange, and the red. See all seven energy centers spinning together in perfect harmony, energy moving up and down the spinal column very easily, very freely.

Now move up above your head, 12 inches above your head. See the magenta spinning energy. See that magenta spinning in perfect harmony with the seven chakras in the body. Move out into Earth's atmosphere. See pink spinning energy. The pink is spinning in perfect harmony with the magenta, the violet, the indigo, the blue, the green, the yellow, the orange, and the red. Move out now to the edge of our solar system. See the turquoise spinning energy. The turquoise is spinning in perfect harmony with the pink, the magenta, the violet, the indigo, the blue, the green, yellow, orange, and red. Move out now to the edge of our galaxy. See gold spinning energy. The gold is spinning in perfect harmony with the turquoise, the pink, the magenta, the violet, the indigo, the blue, the green, the yellow, the orange, and the red. Move out now to the edge of the universe. See the silver spinning energy. The silver is spinning in perfect harmony with the gold, the turquoise, the pink, the magenta, the violet, the indigo, the blue, the green, the yellow, the orange, and the red. From an observer perspective, see your body connected fully with the Earth. See it fully connected to the solar system, fully connected to our galaxy, and fully connected to the universe, to Source. You are one and the same.

See all of those energy centers spinning in perfect harmony with each other. Allow us to now bring in the 12 strands of the DNA to be activated today. Go inside one of your cells. All of your cells are connected. Go inside one of your cells. Go inside the nucleus to where your double-strand DNA resides. See that twisted ladder, the double helix spiral. Know that you are fully connected to Source now. Your cells are all connected to Source.

Coming down from that silver chakra through all of those energy centers, see the third strand coming down. The third one connects to the double helix. Now the fourth one is coming down through those chakras, uniting with the other three. See the fifth one coming down now through those chakras, five strands bonding together. Pull down the sixth one now through those chakras, coming down from Source, forming a bond with the other five. Pull down the seventh one, coming all the way through those chakra centers, uniting with the other six. Now, pull down the eighth strand. See it come down through the chakras, uniting with the other seven. Now, pull down the ninth strand and see it connect with the other eight, all the way down through the chakras, bonding together. Pull down the tenth one now, all the way down through those colored chakras and uniting with the other nine. The eleventh one is coming down from Source, all the way down through the chakras. See it bond with the other ten. Now the twelfth strand is coming down from Source, down through silver, gold, turquoise, pink, magenta, violet, indigo, blue, green, yellow, orange, and red, right into the DNA and combining with the other eleven.

Visualize this twelve-strand DNA. This twelve-strand DNA is activating within your body. This activation gives you super psychic abilities. It allows you to remember your connection to Source. It allows you to know your connection to everything in this universe, to each other, to every living being, every crystal, every tree, and every animal. All things that exist are connected to Source. Allow your body to heal itself, as it has this natural ability. Activating these twelve strands allows that healing to happen much faster. It allows you to release any stuck trauma, any stuck emotions, that keep healing from occurring. See your body from an observer perspective. See it as vibrating golden cells, trillions of cells, vibrating together in perfect harmony with each other. Imagine these cells vibrating faster and faster, increasing your frequency and vibration, shifting into higher dimensions, as you are now ready to meet your Mantis being.

In front of you, see a doorway. Move towards the door and move through the door. Now you're inside a room where you see two chairs. Go sit yourself down in one of those chairs. Look across at the chair that's there. Now, over from where the doorway is, a gray shimmering mist is starting to form. That gray mist is getting thicker and thicker, and it's starting to twirl around. It's starting to move into the room, twirling all around the space, twirling around you, feeling like a warm cozy blanket. You know this mist is safe. You are safe. You are secure, feeling very at peace in this gray mist. One or more of your Mantis guides is coming through the door now, through the mist. The mist is starting to clear, and there will be one or more Mantis beings in front of you. Perhaps one is sitting in the chair. If there are multiple, they might be standing. Get a sense of if this is simply an aspect of you. Perhaps it's one of your family. Perhaps it's just a guide. Look into those very large eyes of this Mantis being. Receive the love that this Mantis has for you. Feel the ancient wisdom that this Mantis has brought.

Receive the message that this Mantis has brought for you today. What ancient wisdom do they wish to share with you today? It may come through telepathy or words. You may see images. Allow their ancient wisdom message to come to you now. They also brought a gift for you today. Hold your hands out and receive the gift they brought you. It may be something that you understand. You may not. Receive the gift now. See it clearly. Ask them what *the purpose of this gift is for you today in this space. Why this gift? Thank them for their message and for the gift.*

Ask them if they have a name that they would like to be called. Some of them will. Some of them won't. Some names are easy to understand. Some are more challenging. Don't judge the name. Just let it come to you now.

As you are sitting across from this Mantis being, feel the energy of the divine masculine that resides within this Mantis being. This divine masculine is also residing in you, no matter what your gender as an Earth human. You have aspects of the feminine and the masculine. Now we're going to call that energy in of the divine masculine with that Mantis in front of you, acting as a mirror. See yourself becoming one with the Mantis. Perhaps your body is changing form into a Mantis. Integrate with this Mantis to feel the energy of the divine masculine. Feel the energy of personal power, self-confidence, success, self-esteem, being able to make decisions easily, and having warrior energy. Bring that divine masculine energy into your body now. Feel the expansion of your solar plexus, that yellow energy center, feeling the power rise up within you. Know how worthy you are. Feel confident in your ability to move through this world easily, without barriers. As you continue to feel this frequency of the solar plexus, having integrated with the Mantis, see out of their eyes. See from their perspective, from this place of higher ancient wisdom.

Pull forth what you wrote down earlier that you want to create in your reality, that symbol you drew to represent that creation. Pull this image up now. See it through the eyes of the Mantis, the manifestor. Hold that image, that symbol, in your mind's eye. Feel how it feels to have manifested that reality. See the symbol, knowing it has already been created. It has already been activated coming down from Source. All things are possible. As this energy is manifesting in front of you, how does it feel in your body? Hold the energy of this feeling of having created your reality. Consciously see it and feel it in your body. Feel your full personal power; the success of having this be manifested now. Hold that image. See it. See it glowing like a laser light. Whatever symbol you drew, see it in your mind. Know it is manifesting right now, right here. Feel it in your body. What does it feel like knowing you are worthy of manifesting this reality? You have the confidence that it is done. It has been created. Keep holding that vision in your mind. The more you hold that focus, the more you feel that energy in your body, and the quicker it will manifest into this Earth life.

Imagine what you have just created. We are now in that timeline where it exists. Take some steps forward in that timeline and see how that new reality plays out for you. Move forward in that timeline where it has been created. See if there are any modifications that you wish to make. You have the ability to create your reality at any time you choose. If you see something you *wish to modify now, simply make that decision. Have the confidence to shift into that reality where you are now, modifying it. You may not need to modify it. You have full conscious, creation power within you. This is something that we are here to remind you of. You have the ability to manifest your reality, to create your reality. You don't need to understand the process of how it is occurring. You just need to see it as if it's done and feel it as if it is done.*

Pull yourself back into the room where the chair is. See a bed in that room. There's a bed that you're going to go lie down on. Observe your body lying down on this bed. There is a Mantis being there with you in the space that is scanning your body. Notice any place in your body that needs some attention for healing energy. You will know it, as the Mantis is scanning your body. Allow the frequency to help shift that. Release whatever patterns, emotions, stuck energy, or physical illness. The magic of the Mantis, master healer, will help you remove all these things stuck in your body. See white light coming down into your body and removing anything that no longer serves you. See this Mantis over your body, scanning it, sending you energy. Keep running that white light through your body. Know that you have activated your twelve strands of DNA, which will help this healing occur much faster than you are normally used to. The energy will continue working through your body for the rest of the day and as you sleep. Know that you can always call on your Mantis for additional healing. Any time you feel your body or your emotions off kilter, all you need to do is simply ask, and it will be given. Go ahead and sit up in the bed. Walk back over to the chair. Once again, see this Mantis being sitting across from you. Receive a final parting message from this Mantis. Let it come to you now.

We are so very happy to connect with you today. We want you to know how much we love you, how much we are always there with you. You may call on us whenever you need anything in terms of healing. If you need extra support in manifesting whatever your reality wants to be, you can call on us. Call in our energy. Remember that you have the power within you to create whatever reality it is. We want you to remember that you are connected to everything. You are always connected to us. You are one of us. You are connected to Source. There is no separation. You have the ability to use all of your powers that are naturally given to you in this human body. You just simply must remember that you have these abilities, and that is what we are here to remind you of today.

Journal prompt:

Take a few moments to write down what you experienced.

Write down the feelings you had and the energy you received.

What did your Mantis look like?

What message did you receive from the Mantis?

What gift did you receive?

What was the experience of aligning your 12 chakras and calling forth your 12-strand DNA?

How did it feel to access the divine masculine within?

What did you manifest?

What did you heal?

Chapter 10

Orions

Who are the Orions?

The Orion constellation is home to many different races and forms. Some are humanoid, while others are Grays, Reptilians, and numerous others. Different groups of Orions have interacted with Earth for various reasons. Ancient Egypt has a strong connection to Orion, as depicted in the alignment of the great pyramids with Orion's belt. Egyptian God Osiris, among others, comes from the Orion system.

The Orion constellation, seeding from Sirius, Lyra, and Vega, became the main battleground in the galaxy for the integration of polarity. The negative side perpetuated "service to self," which led to domination, genetic manipulation of bloodlines, and black magic. The positive side was about "service to others," even at the expense of themselves.

The Orions evolved into a state of technological advancement while still in intense spiritual conflict. The book and movie series, *Star Wars*, is the memory of this conflict brought forth to our awareness. This was a time in history known as the Orion Wars.

Some positive Orions escaped from the Orion Matrix and incarnated on Earth, entering Earth's reincarnation cycle. They were unconsciously playing out the Orion drama in their soul pattern. Some negative Orions also entered the Earth cycle, bringing with them the desire for control. The Fall of Atlantis, the Roman Empire, the Nazis, and ongoing religious wars are examples of memory patterns from Orion, which are here on Earth to be cleared.

At some point in the Orion history, after generations of conflict, a soul incarnated, known as the Orion Christ. He helped them to integrate positivity and negativity to the balance point, demonstrating one must love, not fear. Contemporary Orion has healed its conflict. Integrated Orions moved outward in the galaxy for a fresh start. Some came to Earth where Free Will/Choice was the primary tool.

The energy and wisdom of the Orions include:

Equality

Higher perspective

Inspiration

Integration

Stones/crystals to help you connect:

labradorite, moss agate, green jade, citrine, and hematite (and any other stones that you are called to work with)

Journal prompt:

Where do you experience polarity?

What do you judge?

Where do you feel "right" over someone else?

What have you fought for in your life that you are still fighting?

Summary of the Orion Journey

In this session, the Orions take you on a journey to observe Earth from a higher perspective to understand the polarity and how it separates people and creates judgment of others who are different. They guide you to explore the lives of those different from you so you understand things from a different perspective. They encourage you to integrate your own polarity into your Earth life and to stay out of judgment.

The induction part of the journey to raise your vibration and activate your DNA has been omitted. Please refer to Chapter 2 for the process to get yourself into a higher vibrational state of mind.

Journey to Meet Your Orion

In front of you is a door. Walk towards the door, and on the other side of the door is a room with two comfy chairs. You're now through the door, seeing the two comfy chairs facing each other. Go sit down in one of the chairs. Over by the doorway, see a shimmering gray mist starting to form around the door. The gray mist is getting thicker and thicker and thicker, allowing your Orion family or guides or perhaps even an aspect of yourself to come through that gray mist to be with you today. The mist is starting to get a little bit thinner. Start making out shapes coming through the door. There may be one or more beings coming into this space. You now have clear vision of how many are there with you. Invite one of them to sit down in the chair. Get a very clear image of what they look like. If there are multiple beings, are they all the same form, or do they have diversity among them?

Take a look very deeply at what they look like, the one in the chair in front of you. Do they have a head that we would be familiar with and a body that we would be familiar with? What does their head look like? Do they have hair or not? Take a look at the shape of their head and the size of their head. How big is it in relationship to their body? Take a look at their skin color. What color do you see? Look into their eyes. What do their eyes look like? How big are they? What shape are they? What color are they? Take a look at their other facial features. Do they have a nose or mouth, and what do those look like if so? Do they have ears that you can see or not?

Take a look at their body. Are they wearing any kind of clothing or not? What feelings do you get from them? Is this a family member? Is it a guide or an aspect of yourself that you're looking at? Let that answer come. If there are multiple beings, take a look at them again. Do they have the same form, or do they differ in what they look like? Some of you may have an entire team. There are some of you that may have just one. Whatever it is, it's perfectly fine.

They came with a message for you today, something that you need to understand from their wisdom as an Orion being. This message may come through words, *through telepathy, or images. Allow yourself to receive their message now.*

They came with a gift for you today. Holding your hands out, receive the gift they brought for you. You may understand what it is. You may not. Receive the gift, seeing it clearly. Ask them the purpose or meaning of this gift they brought for you today for this time and space. Why this gift now? What does it represent? Allow that information to come to you now.

Ask them if they have a name that they would like to be called. Some of them will. Some of them won't. Some names they give are very easy to understand. Others are more challenging. If they have a name, receive it now.

Now that they are there with you, they want to take you on a journey. Take their hands into your hands. Look deep into their eyes, looking into the window to their soul. Feel the energy of who they are, the wisdom that they carry. Allow yourself to be transported in time, space, and dimension with them to see how they see things from a higher perspective. As you're holding their hands, over to the side of the room, a spaceship now appears. Walk with them towards the spaceship. Enter the spaceship. Don't worry about the physics of it. Just enter the spaceship.

Now, you are sitting very comfortably in this spaceship. It takes off, and it's flying through time, space, and dimension. Look out the window. See the darkness of space. See the star points; how beautiful this vast darkness with tiny points of light is. The spacecraft is arriving just outside of Earth's atmosphere. Look down on Earth, just like you're an astronaut observing it from that higher perspective. See the beautiful colors of Earth, the blue water, the green and brown continents, the white of the clouds, this beautiful marble of Mother Gaia with all of her diversity.

Observing from this higher perspective, imagine Earth as an amusement park, perhaps like Epcot Center, where the different continents, the different countries, represent different experiences, different rides you can go on. As the Earth is rotating, see how many opportunities there are to be Earth human. See how many opportunities there are to play different roles and to have different experiences.

Now, still observing from this higher perspective, look at the North American continent. See it from a higher perspective. See the United States as the melting pot where diversity is plenty, similar to the Orion system. All different types of people are living among each other, having different opinions, different ideas, and different information they are willing to receive and integrate into their lives. Just observe without judgment some of the polarities currently happening in this country, in this United States. The religious dramas that are going on, the righteous, the political dramas that are going on, just observe it.

See that it's simply a game, like a video game, where people are taking on different avatars to play out different experiences and gain different wisdom. Do your best to just observe, again without judgment, accepting everyone for the choices they are making, coming from a place of love. Understand from this higher perspective that there truly is no right or wrong. All experiences are valid. All experiences are choices to be made. One has the opportunity to make different choices, whether within a particular life or for the next life they might choose to live.

Now move down closer. Pull up in your mind one of the types of judgment or polarity you might be experiencing in your current Earth human life. Imagine yourself being in the body of the person opposite you, with opposite ideas. Place yourself in their body, with their brain, with their understanding of how they grew up. Understand how they might have come to the perspective that they carry, not that it is right or wrong. There is no right or wrong. Just understand how someone might not understand what your real side of things is, what you feel judgmental about or righteous about.

Now move out of that body and put yourself back into your Earth human body with that understanding. See that not everyone has all the information they need to make informed decisions and to make non-judgmental decisions because they are experiencing deeply this Earth polarity. Now, you have a choice to either engage with them or to stay above it. There is no right or wrong, so if you choose to engage with them, we want you to understand that the push-pull will continue. It must. Again, there is no right or wrong in this. Imagine yourself not engaging with that polarized person opposite you, pulling yourself out of it, above it. Imagine yourself sending them love. Just send them love from your heart. When you are coming in from that love vibration, it allows the judgment to melt away. You get to choose whether or not you want to be in that experience.

The more you can keep yourself out of the polarity, out of the judgment, the more your vibration is vibrating higher. You are more closely aligning yourself to fifth-dimensional reality, which is where Earth is headed, where humanity is headed. At that fifth-dimensional level, there is no more judgment. There is no more good or bad. You understand that you are one and the same as that person that you were formally opposite from, polarized from. They're simply just a different expression of you. The more you can integrate that into your daily Earth life, the more your vibration will stay in a high place. You will experience more joy in your life, in flow, easier. The struggle will no longer need to be there. It's when you are pushing that the struggle occurs.

We want you to see this from this higher perspective. All timelines exist simultaneously. There are timelines where that polarity is lessened, even in this Earth plane. We invite you to stay out of the judgment, to understand the balance of the universe, the balance of the polarity. We want you to understand the connection you have to all Earth humans, whether you like them or agree with them or not.

Now pulling yourself once again above Earth's atmosphere back into the spaceship, see the Earth rotating. See yourself now floating down to Asia. Land in someone's body that resides on the Asian continent. It doesn't matter which country. Experience seeing through their eyes what their life is like and perhaps understanding what lessons they came to learn, what wisdom they are gaining, and why they might have chosen that particular life. Understand we all choose what life we experience. Again, just like at an amusement park, you get to choose which rides you go on. Some of you love the roller coasters, the emotional butterflies in your stomach as you go up and down and twirl around. Others of you like to play it a little safer. Again, there is no right or wrong, or good or bad. Just like at the amusement park, you are getting to choose the experiences that will evolve you and feed information back to Source to provide new information and new perspectives. It is all a game. When you understand it is a game, you have more control over your reality and more control over your life. You understand you create your reality.

Go ahead and pull yourself out of that Asian body experience. Earth is rotating, and now you're landing somewhere in Africa, experiencing the life of some type of African person. Perhaps it's great wealth. Perhaps it's extreme poverty or somewhere in between. See life from those eyes, from that experience. Understand again, it's just simply a choice, a new role to play.

Pull yourself up out of that African body. Earth is rotating once again and now landing in South America. Put yourself into the body of someone in South America, whatever the experience you might want to have. Perhaps it's high in the mountains or deep in the jungles. Just see what that life is like. What is it like to live that life? It's just another choice, another ride to go on.

Now pull yourself up out of the South American life, back on the spacecraft where you can see Earth and all her beauty. Watch it like you might a TV show or a movie. See all of these different experiences playing out, billions of people on this planet having different experiences that they have all chosen. They have all chosen the roles they want to be. The people in their lives have chosen the roles they're going to play out for those people. Some are victims, martyrs, tortured, or in poverty. Some are the complete flip side of that. Some are tyrants, have the control, and have all of the money. It's simply a game. See *it from a higher perspective. Allow people to live what they came here on Earth to live. That is what we invite you to do.*

Now that you see it from this higher perspective, you might understand how to integrate your own polarity and how to create your own equality and balance in your life. Holding yourself in this higher frequency allows you to do that. Stay out of anything that is of lower vibration. That is a fear that is holding you back. It no longer serves you unless you want it to. You have the opportunity to break out of the karmic cycle that you may be stuck in. It's simply a choice. At this time, you can simply say, I am done. I have completed whatever karma I have come here to experience. I am no longer bound by the rules of the karmic cycle. You create your reality.

As you're looking down on Earth, just observing humanity, observing the experiences, open your heart once again. Send the green heart love energy down onto Earth, beaming green down onto Earth. Allow the heart chakra frequency to carry that green energy to permeate all Earth humans. Let them feel the love frequency you carry as it's generated within you.

Each one of you carries this love frequency. You have a choice whether you want to send that out or keep it for yourself. Each one of you has the ability to make major changes here on Earth, to share your love energy, to be the light for those around you, in your network, your sphere of influence. You are here because you are ready to hear this message, pull yourself out of the fight, and focus on the future, the new Earth, the integrated Earth where there is no more judgment. Polarity dissolves because there is understanding, allowing, and acceptance. This starts with you.

We invite you to stop judging yourself and stop fighting with yourself. Come from a place of love. See yourself as love, being love. The more you experience yourself as love, that emanates out into your environment. There will no longer be the conflicts you might have previously experienced. Only that which is frequency specific to you of that love energy can come into your space. You get to choose whether you have drama or not. Perhaps there might be remnants of wanting to get caught up in the emotional cycle of the drama. Humans get addicted to their emotions. It's simply a matter of having enough space away from those emotions to break the habit. It is a practice. The more you practice this, the more beautiful and peaceful your life will be. The more harmony you will have.

Now, the spaceship is flying back to the room. Once again, see yourself sitting across from the Orion that came to be with you today, whether it's the one or it's the group of them. Receive a final message from them. They want to share with you from their perspective. Receive their message now. Thank them for coming to you today, *to be with you today. Know you can always call on them when you need their extra support, their energy, and their wisdom. Whenever you feel yourself in a polarized moment, tap into their energy. Allow them to help raise your vibration above the judgment and to be in the place of love.*

Journal prompt:

Take a few moments to write down what you experienced.

Write down the feelings you had and the energy you received.

What did your Orion look like?

What was their message?

What gift did you receive?

What was the experience of seeing Earth as an amusement park?

How did your perspective change when you were in the bodies of people so different from you?

Are you willing to let go of judgment of others?

Are you ready to let go of the judgment of yourself?

Chapter 11

Pleiadians

Who are the Pleiadians?

Pleiadians are humanoid and indistinguishable from Nordic Earth humans. Their skin is light, but their hair color ranges from light to dark. The Pleiades constellation was colonized first by Lyran humanoid offshoots, who initially went to Earth before moving to Pleiades. A group of Lyrans went to Earth and became an Earth-Lyran race, colonizing the area of Scandinavia. They incorporated primate genetics into themselves to assimilate better to Earth's environment. A different group of Lyrans was on Earth simultaneously, inserting Lyran genetics into primates, creating a conflict between the two groups.

The Earth-Lyrans left Earth to go to the Pleiades, where they wanted to create a culture based on harmony, truth, and unconditional love. They were living the intuitive feminine polarity. Other Lyrans began to colonize the Pleiades, attracted by the desire to create a community lifestyle. They evolved at a healthy rate, balancing their philosophical/spiritual nature with technology, and were stable for thousands of years.

The Lyrans asked some of the Pleiadians to return to Earth due to their terrestrial DNA becoming the primary genetic connection from non-Earth sources for humans. They were directly involved with the development of the Earth human species. They spent thousands of years interacting with most of the primitive cultures on Earth. Ancient documents, drawings, and carvings on cave walls and rocks record this interaction of the "gods." They played a massive role in Lemuria and islands and countries of the Pacific Ocean, including Easter Island, Hawaii, Micronesia, Indonesia, New Zealand, Australia, and Japan.

Although contact with the Pleiadians has slowed down in modern times compared to the past, they are here to assist humanity. They are the most similar to Earth humans physically and genetically. They are generally depicted as Nordic-looking.

The energy and wisdom of the Pleiadians include:

Compassion

Divine Feminine

Empathy

Growth

Stones/crystals to help you connect:

strawberry quartz, rose quartz, larimar, blue calcite, blue aventurine, amazonite, and other light pink and blue stones (and any other stones that you are called to work with)

Journal prompt:

Where do you hold onto judgment of yourself?

What would it feel like to release trying to prove your worth?

Do you have compassion and empathy for others?

Summary of the Pleiadian Journey

In this session, the Pleiadians guide you through an experience to see things through their perspective. They fully activate the divine feminine within you. They allow you to feel what it is like to be in a harmonious community, with empathy and compassion for yourself and others.

The induction part of the journey to raise your vibration and activate your DNA has been omitted. Please refer to Chapter 2 for the process to get yourself into a higher vibrational state of mind.

Journey to Meet Your Pleiadian

See a door in front of you. Move through the door into a room with two very comfy chairs. Go sit down in one of the comfy chairs that is directly across from another comfy chair. Sit in this room feeling so completely relaxed. You know that you are safe. Be excited about who is going to come through this door. One or more of the Pleiadians is walking towards you, with one of them sitting in the chair.

Clearly see who is sitting in front of you. Take a look at their features. Take a look at what color their hair is. How long is their hair? Look at their face. Look into their eyes. What color are their eyes? Really stare into those eyes, the window to the soul. Feel the love this Pleiadian has for you.

Receive a message from this Pleiadian who has come to be in this space with you, in this time and space. It may come through words. It may come through telepathy or as images. Go ahead and receive the message now.

They brought a gift for you as well. Hold your hands out and receive the gift the Pleiadian has brought you today, in this time and space, in this room. Get a good visual on what this gift is. You may already understand the meaning of it, but if not, ask the Pleiadian what the meaning of this gift is for you, in this time and space, in this room. What does the gift represent? Allow that answer to come to you now.

Ask them if they have a name they want to be called. Some of them will, some of them won't. If they have a name, receive it now. If it's something you can't understand, then ask them to try to either spell it out or give you something you can understand. Thank them for the message they've given you, for the gift they've given you, and for their name.

Take their hands in your hands. The chairs are close enough. Be close enough to them that your knees are touching. You're holding their hands. Stare into their eyes. As you're holding their hands, knees touching, staring into their eyes, feel the love that they have for you, this beautiful unconditional love. Feel the energy coming from their heart moving into your heart, becoming one, that energy link. You're connected by the hands. You're connected with your eyes. You're connected in your heart space. Feel this love. Feel this connection.

See yourself becoming this Pleiadian. See the Pleiadian being as a mirror of you. As you look at yourself as a Pleiadian, send love to them. Send this love energy to their heart space, this unconditional love. Feel compassion for this mirror image of yourself. See yourself sitting across from you; so much love. See yourself as whole and complete, having no judgment about you as you are sitting across from yourself in this space, in this time. Know that you are perfect and whole just the way that you are.

As you're sitting across from yourself, the Pleiadian, it's time to dive deep into your intuition, to trust that part of you, to allow yourself to rise up in the divine feminine of that which you are. No matter your sex as this Earth human right now, see yourself and that part of you that is truly divine. Know you are perfect and whole just as you are. Feel the power of that feminine side. Know you are able to nurture, not only nurture yourself but nurture those in your world. You have compassion for yourself first and foremost, and with that, then you are able to have compassion for others around you. You have empathy for yourself, getting over any judgment you have about any part of yourself.

Really see yourself for who and what you are. Love all aspects of that without judgment. In doing so, you are able to have empathy for others around you, without judgment, understanding everyone has their own jour-

ney. See your timeline and how you have grown in this human life, from being born to going through being a toddler, childhood, teenage years, going through your early adult years, perhaps into mid-life, and now later life. Really see and appreciate how much you have grown. You may have been stuck at times, but you are still here. You are still showing up for yourself, and that is what matters. Appreciate all the parts of your life, the good and the bad times. In those bad times, you learned things. You gained wisdom. Fully appreciate all of this beautiful Earth life you came here to live.

Know that you are whole and complete in yourself. Look at the different parts of your life without judgment, shame, or guilt. Know you chose to come into this life with these experiences you've had. If you are a woman at this time, know you came here to be part of this divine feminine rising. If you're male in this life, you also came to be part of this time of the divine feminine rising. We have been stuck in the patriarchy for far too long. It's not about one being superior to the other. It's about being in balance, in community, and in harmony with each other.

It's time to rise up, to stand fully powerful in your feminine side. Whether you are male or female, it does not matter. We have all aspects within us. See yourself as this beautiful divine feminine aspect that fully trusts your intuition. You have the ability to nurture yourself *and others. You have that kind, compassionate, loving heart to truly serve others without sacrificing yourself in the meantime. Boundaries are great. Even with boundaries in place, when we serve ourselves from a place of love, we fill our cups. We have so much love and generosity to give to others.*

Imagine yourself in a time and place on Earth where you are in total harmony with the environment around you, with the community around you. There is no power. There is no control. There is love and understanding and compassion. There is no duality in terms of good or bad or right or wrong. See what this harmonious community looks like. Feel it in your body as if it is the truth of your life. This is where we are headed into fifth-dimensional reality from the third dimension.

The more you can see this harmony, this community, the sharing, the loving, the compassion, the more you can see this and feel this, it allows you to move into that timeline where you exist in this fifth-dimensional reality space. All timelines exist simultaneously. This is where you are headed. This is who you are evolving to be. It's time to release anything that is not serving you. It's time to release judgments. It's time to release any anger or frustration over this Earth system. Sometimes, things have to get a little darker before they get brighter. That is what we see happening now on this Earth. We do not want you to be discouraged. Earth is evolving, and there is no turning back from that. Earth is shifting into her fifth-dimensional reality, and you are part of that.

Part of that experience is truly stepping into the divine feminine. Don't let anything keep you from fully showing up in your beautiful, feminine, intuitive side. The systems are changing. They're falling away. While that may be uncomfortable for a short while, it allows an opportunity for new growth, new experience, and new evolution and for us to become a harmonious community serving each other. Because we are fully filled in ourselves, there is no more competition. It is a true collaboration, and the women are the leaders of that. They are showing the way of how to be that compassion, that nurturing, that loving energy. They give permission for all of the men to express that in themselves. No more shaming the men. It's time for them to change as well, to step into their divine feminine side. As you hold this vision, allow the energy to fill your body with the frequency of love. Let it move out any kind of emotion that is no longer serving you.

With regards to women or the patriarchy, hold that vision of a harmonious community. Feel that love energy pulsing through your body, knowing this is who you are. You are loved, and you have love to give to the world. You are worthy. You are love. You are supported in so many ways and by so many outside entities and inside entities, more than you can ever imagine. Whenever *you doubt yourself and your feminine energy and your intuition, whenever you are not feeling so worthy of yourself, you can call on us, the Pleiadians. We will help you with that energy. You can tap into that image of that fifth-dimensional harmonious reality because that is real. That exists. That is where we reside, as well as in higher states. We love you so very much.*

Coming back out of that environment, once again go back to the room with the chair. Across from you, in the other chair, is you as a tiny child, an innocent, pure child. Bring this child onto your lap. Hug this child. Embrace this child and tell this child how much you love them, how worthy they are, this beautiful little child that is you. Fill this child up with all of the love you have. Look into this tiny child's eyes and feel the pure love they have for you without judgment. Look at them and see how beautiful, how innocent they are without judgment. See your bodies vibrating faster and faster, where your energy is becoming one with each other. This child is becoming a part of you, no longer separate. All of the love you gave this child is deep inside you now. This is your self-love, your self-worthiness. Learn to trust your intuition. You have all of the answers, all of the wisdom, inside you. Allow yourself to trust that fully.

Journal prompt:

Take a few moments to write down what you experienced.

Write down the feelings you had and the energy you received.

What did your Pleiadian look like?

What was their message?

What gift did you receive?

What was the experience of being fully in the divine feminine power?

How did it feel to be in total harmony with your community?

What can you do to embrace your self-love and worthiness?

Chapter 12

Reptilians

Who are the Reptilians?

The Reptilians, including the Draconians, are a controversial and misunderstood group. They often get lumped into one category or are believed to be one race. However, countless Reptilian races come from all different star systems within our galaxy and beyond, including but not limited to Lyra, Sirius, Orion, Inner Earth, and Draco. Some Reptilian and Draconian groups have individuals who are "service to self," while others are "service to others." They are not all "negative" in the way they are portrayed. Those in fourth density (fifth dimension) and above understand love and unity and have evolved beyond polarity.

Humanoid Vegans who first came to Earth during the time of the early dinosaurs incorporated reptile DNA into themselves to create a mammalian species with reptilian features. Other Vegan individuals incorporated even more reptilian DNA into their bodies to create a species with more reptilian qualities than mammalian. These Earth-based Reptilians, described as raptor-like, are one of the groups who have gone inside of the Earth to live.

Reptilians have interacted with many of Earth's ancient cultures. There are Reptilians depicted in statues from ancient Sumeria. Egyptian gods with reptilian appearance include Sobek, Ammut, Wadjet, Apep, Renenutet, Nehebkau, and others. In India and the East, the Naga are serpentine gods. Dragons, a type of Reptilian, are depicted all over the world. In the Mayan culture, Quetzalcóatl is a serpent-like Reptilian. In Polynesian culture, the Mo'o Wahine are lizard women that resemble mermaids. In Australia, the Rainbow Serpent is the primary creator god. This is just a small sampling of Reptilian influence on Earth.

Reptilians come in many different forms, just as we have a diversity of reptiles on Earth. They appear with varying degrees of reptile/humanoid form as dinosaurs, crocodiles, snakes, lizards, and dragons.

The energy and wisdom of the Reptilians include:

Adaptability

Confident

Self-Power

Transformation

Stones/crystals to help you connect:

dragon blood stone, red jasper, red agate, carnelian, obsidian, clear quartz, citrine, labradorite (and any other stones that you are called to work with)

Journal prompt:

Where would you like to transform your life?

How do you adapt to changes? Easily? With hardship?

Where could you use more confidence and self-power in your life?

Summary of the Reptilian Journey

In this session, the Reptilians allow you to merge with their energy to understand things from their perspective. As you are in their body, you experience the shedding of what no longer serves you and how adaptable you are to your environment. You understand their confidence and self-power. They introduce you to a dragon friend that allows you to ride on its back to take you above situations to see them from a higher perspective.

The induction part of the journey to raise your vibration and activate your DNA has been omitted. Please refer to Chapter 2 for the process to get yourself into a higher vibrational state of mind.

Journey to Meet Your Reptilian

In front of you is a door. Go ahead and walk towards the door. Move through the door. On the other side of this door is a room with two very comfy chairs facing each other. Sit down in one of these comfy chairs. Notice a gray mist starting to form around the door. You know this mist is safe. Through this mist, you now have one or more of your Reptilians coming into the room. Allow yourself to see this Reptilian coming and sitting down in the chair.

Have clear vision now of what they look like. See what this Reptilian looks like. Notice how many there are with you. If there is more than one, look at all of them. Are they the same kind? Are they different? For the one sitting in the chair opposite you, look at this Reptilian's head. Notice what kind of eyes this Reptilian has. What color are these eyes? What is the shape of the head? Does it have a long, pointed snout or a shorter snout? Does it look a little more human? What kind of reptile face would you most liken it to? What color is the skin of this Reptilian?

Notice what the scales might look like. Are they small? Are they large? Perhaps it looks more like human skin. Whatever you're seeing is perfectly fine. Now look down at the body. Does your Reptilian have more of a human-shaped kind of body being bipedal? Or is it quadrupedal, more like reptiles here on Earth? Perhaps it has wings. Perhaps it's more snake-like without limbs. Get a really good visual on what the body of your Reptilian looks like. Does it have any clothing that it's wearing, or not? If it does have clothing, look at what this clothing might look like. Allow yourself to see these details.

Look deep into the eyes of this Reptilian. Feel their energy. Feel their love, knowing that they are a higher dimensional Reptilian. Is this one of your family? Is it one of your guides? Is it an aspect of yourself? Know this answer now.

This Reptilian came with a message for you today in this space, in this time and place. Receive their message. It may come through words, telepathy, or images. Receive the message now. This Reptilian brought a gift for you today. Hold your hands out. Receive the gift they brought, seeing it clearly and feeling it in your hands. Feel the physicalness of it. You may understand what the gift represents already. You may not. Ask them now to tell you what this gift means for you in this time and space. Allow that answer to come to you now.

Ask them if they have a name that they would like to be called. Some of them will. Some of them won't. Some names are very easy. Others can be more challenging. If they have a name that they want to give you, receive that name now.

Once again, look deep into their eyes. Start merging with them, becoming them. See that you're turning into them in your body, or you are merging into one entity together. See yourself transforming into this Reptilian so that you can know what it knows. You can see what it sees and feel what it feels. As you are in this Reptilian body, notice how your body feels. Does it feel different than being in your human body? Does it feel similar? Notice any sensations happening in your body as you feel into this Reptilian body. Look out of their eyes and see how you might perceive things differently from this higher perspective, this wisdom.

Pull up the thing you wrote down that you are ready or would like to transform in your life. Pull that up in your mind's eye. As this Reptilian in this Reptilian body, you have the ability to shapeshift, to transform into what you desire it to be. See the skin shedding off this Reptilian body, allowing it to emerge into a new experience. The shedding of the layers allows you to get deeper and deeper into your inner wisdom, into what *you still need to heal. As you see your skin shed off this Reptilian body, see the evolution as each layer comes off, getting deeper and deeper. See yourself transform into the new reality you would like to create. Perhaps your body changes form. It might just be a situation in your life. Whatever it is, allow that to come. Feel it in your body, this transformation that's happening. See how the perception of your environment changes as you're shedding these layers. Release what no longer serves you, letting go of the past. Only focus on the present and what you are transforming into now. As your body has transformed, your situation has transformed.*

In this new environment, see how adaptable you are to this environment. How do you respond from this higher perspective? Do you feel more in control of your responses, as this Reptilian energy? You have the ability to adapt very quickly to new situations in a beautiful way, easily. It does not have to be challenging. It just naturally happens. It's who you are. It's how you were made to operate. This is just like a chameleon, which has the ability to change its coloration based on the environment, and other Earth-based reptiles, which are able to change their temperature naturally without even trying.

With this Reptilian energy, you have the ability to adapt in your life in the way that you want to, going with the flow rather than fighting against the current. You can pull this energy in as an idea, a concept, or a reality because it is part of who you are. You have this Reptilian DNA inside of you. It's now activated. Your body has the ability to respond now beautifully to your environment. It is up to you to put yourself in an environment that supports you for your highest and greatest good if that is what you want your outcome to be. That will allow your transformation to happen very quickly.

Now you're in this new reality, this new environment. This transformation has occurred. Feel how much confidence you have knowing that you are able to transform yourself and transform your reality. Feel that confidence of having done it, feeling that in your body. Know that whatever might come to you in your life, you can pull that confidence up to know that you can achieve whatever it is you want to achieve.

Feel how powerful you are. You make things happen in your reality. You consciously create your reality, which gives you power over your life and power over your situations. This is not power over other people; however, this is self-power. Your self-power allows you to do amazing things you may not have ever considered you could do. Feel this power within you, this knowingness that you can adapt. You can transform. You create your reality. You have the ability with this self-power to speak up for yourself, to ask for what you desire. It does not matter what others around you may think about what you are requesting. Be impeccable in how you are calling things into your life without being a tyrant over others. Bring things into your life that you desire with no harm to anyone or anything else.

As you feel this power in your body, allow the expansion of frequency of the solar plexus, the power center. This energy vibrates within every cell of your body, making it so, bringing this power in. Feel this power in every cell of your body. Feel the confidence that it brings to you. Trust yourself now as you feel this power within your body and confidence within your mind.

Across from you now is a dragon friend. Look into the dragon's eyes. This may be a dragon that you already know. It may be one that's new to you. See what color this dragon is that's in front of you. Notice what its scales look like and what its body looks like. What kind of wings does it have? This is your dragon that will allow you to see things from a higher perspective, as your Earth human.

Climb up onto the back of this dragon. Sit on the dragon. Now, the dragon is taking off into the air. Feel the breeze on your face as this dragon is flying through the air. You're completely safe on this dragon. Look back down at the ground from which this dragon and you were on, seeing from a higher perspective. You are getting higher and higher. As you and the dragon are flying higher into the sky, you gain a much more clear perspective on reality. You understand things from a much higher perspective. You're able to take yourself out of your emotions that might be harming you, such as anxiety, depression, guilt, shame, or fear. Any time you feel any of those emotions and do not want to be in them, acknowledge them and get on your dragon's back. Fly up into the sky, leaving the emotions behind. Allow your body to reset to a neutral place.

From this higher perspective, you can also see how the game is playing out in your life. You can see the moves that other people are making. It gives you the opportunity to respond in a conscious, deliberate way as opposed to unconsciously reacting to them. The more conscious you are, seeing things from this higher perspective, knowing that you have the power within you, it will change your Earth human life in ways you cannot imagine. You will walk through your life with confidence. Allow yourself to have this experience. Know that you can have this experience whenever you choose to.

This dragon that you are on, this is your personal dragon. It is always there for you. You can call on the dragon and the Reptilian you met in the room. You can call in that energy in the experience of shedding the layers, which allows you to evolve and transform into who you really want to be, who you desire to be. It allows you to adapt to your environment much more easily than you may have before this experience.

As you open your crown, take in the energy of this power, this confidence, this knowing that you have the ability to transform and adapt. You have the ability to see things from this higher perspective, which allows you to get out of judgment of yourself and other people. This will help bring you into higher dimensional reality where all of your higher dimensional guides and aspects of yourself are awaiting you to connect with them. There is absolutely nothing to fear of Reptilian energy. Only that which is of the same vibration that you resonate at can come into your space. You have been told this before, and we are the ones who want to remind you of this. Yes, there are always lower vibrating entities, including Earth humans. The higher you can hold your vibration, your frequency, only that which matches that can come into your environment. People will fall away from you as they are meant to.

Remember that you have the power in your life. You have beautiful free will to do what you choose. You just simply must remember to take back that control, that power. That is within you. Nothing can be done to you when you know you have this power unless you decide you want it done.

See your dragon landing back on the ground. Now, walk through that door where the two chairs sit across from each other and once again sit in the chair. See the original Reptilian in front of you. Receive a final parting *message from this Reptilian that came to be with you. Go ahead and receive the message now. Thank this Reptilian or group of them for being with you today.*

Journal prompt:

Take a few moments to write down what you experienced.

Write down the feelings you had and the energy you received.

What did your Reptilian look like?

What was their message?

What gift did you receive?

What did it feel like to shed the layers to allow transformation to occur?

How was it to adapt quickly to your environment?

Could you feel the confidence within your body?

What did you notice as you were flying the back of your dragon?

Chapter 13

Sirians

Who are the Sirians?

Sirians come from the Sirius star system. Some are humanoid in form. Others resemble Grays, Reptilians, and other diverse species and races. Sirius has numerous water planets, giving rise to various aquatic forms. Cetaceans (whales and dolphins) originate from Sirius, as well as other marine life, including sharks, octopods, and merpeople. Life exists in all dimensions in the Sirius system, some physical and others non-physical.

There is a strong Earth connection with the Sirians. They came to Earth to share their knowledge and enhance the physical body of Earth humans. They are strongly connected to ancient Egypt, the Mayan culture, and the Dogon tribe in Africa, as well as others around the globe. In Egypt, they densified their frequency to become visible to third-density humans.

They appeared as the gods and goddesses, including Isis and Anubis. They gave Egyptians and other cultures advanced agricultural, astronomical, and medical information.

Many early Sirians were adept at genetic engineering. The Sirians placed a latent DNA code within early humans during the Earth Inception. When Earth reaches a specific vibratory frequency as a race, the code will be triggered, assisting in the remembrance of our galactic past. Genetic engineering by the Sirians was also used to upgrade the physical human body to hold more energy of a higher frequency.

Sirians help with the physical healing of Earth humans. It is the most widely used energy on Earth. Those physical healers who remained in the Sirius area allied themselves with Arcturus, which carries emotional healing energy. Together, they form the Sirius/Arcturus Matrix, the healing of mind, body, and spirit.

During a Quantum Healing Hypnosis Technique (QHHT) session, I experienced a life as a Sirian. I was one of the genetic engineers who came to Earth to upgrade the human body during the time of very ancient Egypt. The purpose of this was to change the body so that it could hold more energy. As humans are shifting into higher dimensional reality, they need to be able to run more energy through their physical bodies. I observed that the genetic modification was done from our spacecraft using sound frequency vibration coming from the craft. We did not directly interact with the humans when doing this. However, other Sirians from our area were physically on Earth at the same time. These different individuals were teaching the humans how to use sound frequency and thought to levitate the stones to build the pyramids. They were also directly teaching them about agriculture, astronomy, and medicine.

The energy and wisdom of the Sirians include:

Ascension

Joy

Physical healing

Playful

Stones/crystals to help you connect:

green aventurine, green calcite, jade, emerald, larimar, and other green and blue stones (and any other stones that you are called to work with)

Journal prompt:

Where in your body do you have physical tension or illness?

If you could name the root cause, what might it be?

What are you ready to release today?

Summary of the Sirian Journey

In this session, the Sirians guide you through a process to put yourself into an energetic pyramid where your DNA is activated for faster physical healing. Within this higher vibrational environment, the dolphins, whales, and merpeople bring in their wisdom of joy and play.

The induction part of the journey to raise your vibration and activate your DNA has been omitted. Please refer to Chapter 2 for the process to get yourself into a higher vibrational state of mind.

Journey to Meet Your Sirian

See your body as vibrating cells. They're vibrating as golden energy cells, trillions of cells vibrating together in perfect harmony. With your hand, starting at the top of your head, draw a triad shape. Move from your forehead down to one leg. Move the line over from that leg to the other leg, and then move it back up to the top of your forehead, creating a triad, pyramid shape. Now that you know what to do, start at the top of the forehead. Move your hand down very slowly, very consciously. See a laser line in your mind's eye as your hand comes down. You're seeing this line being drawn in your mind down to one of your legs. Then the line makes a very sharp angle, coming straight across to the other leg, very slowly, very consciously. When you are at that point, complete the triad. Consciously, see that laser line with the other two lines already formed. When calling on the Sirian energy, we ask that you create this triad shape to connect with us easier.

Now, inside this triad, visualize your body sitting very comfortably inside this pyramid. Across from you is another Sirian entity. One or multiple beings are now coming into this triad space to be with you today. As you're sitting in this pyramid space, visualize one or more of these Sirian beings that are there to be with you today. Really look into their eyes to feel the energy they bring now. If there are multiple beings with you of different types, take a moment to look at each one. Really look into their eyes. Look into the windows to the soul. Feel their energy. Take in their wisdom, knowing they are a part of you. Get a sense of whether this is just one of your guides. Perhaps it's your family, or it may be another aspect of yourself. All of it is good. There is no wrong.

One of the primary ones that is there with you came with a message for you today. Receive the message they have. Just let it come to you. It may come as telepathy. You may hear it. You may see images. Let their message come to you right now.

They also brought a gift for you. Hold your hands out and receive the gift they have for you. It may be something you understand. You may not. Without judgment, just receive the gift. Ask what the purpose of this gift is for you in this time and space from this Sirian being. What does this gift represent? Allow the answer to come to you, no judgment. Thank them for the message and the gift.

Ask them if they have a name they would like to be called. Some of them will. Some of them won't. It's all okay. If they have a name, receive it now without judgment. It may be something very common that you understand. It may be something you can't even pronounce. Let the name come. Thank them for being here with you.

All of the Sirian beings are surrounding this pyramid that you're inside of. Imagine yourself in the middle of the pyramid. Feel the energy that is coming from this pyramid. Pyramids generate energy. They are healing. You are in the center of this pyramid space where healing can occur. And as you are there inside of the pyramid, once again see your body as vibrating cells, golden energy cells vibrating very high. Go inside one of these cells. Go inside of the nucleus where the DNA resides. See this beautiful DNA structure, this beautiful spiral ladder.

Intuitively, you're going to go to the part of the DNA that is ready to be activated today to not only increase your connection with your Sirian family, but also to activate your body to be able to hold more energy as you expand as you ascend towards fifth-dimensional reality. The DNA you're intuitively at is splitting open. A flash of golden white light energy is moving through the center now. The energy has activated the DNA for a stronger connection. It activates the latent part of the DNA that is part of the Sirian family and has a beautiful ability to heal itself. The body knows how to do this. It just has to remember. Go ahead and see the DNA closing back up. Pull yourself out of the nucleus and out of the cell. Once again, see your body as vibrating energy cells, a golden energy body. As you see your body vibrate, imagine those cells vibrating faster and faster to create a full golden energy body inside this pyramid.

You are more energy than you are physical. When you remember this, this is how you are able to heal your body. Your environment creates how your DNA is expressed. Just because you might have some hereditary DNA of some illness or disease in your family, it does not mean you are destined to express it. You have control over your environment. That is why it is so important to clear out *the trauma and emotions, rewire the brain, and have an environment that supports your body's healing. Your science is now understanding that this is reality.*

As you are in this pyramid space with your golden energy body, it is creating a new environment for your body to live in, allowing it to express new proteins that will restructure the body form. It will remove any illness that you have stuck in your body. Take in this energy now. Allow yourself to continue to be inside of the pyramid. See your golden energy body. Feel the energy coming into your body through the pyramid being amplified. As you are inside of this pyramid, if there are any places in the body where you are feeling tension or you know you have a physical ailment, a physical illness, inside of that golden energy body, visualize where in the body that energy mass is, that physical ailment. See that energy mass dissolving away.

As you're still sitting inside of this pyramid, notice if there is any residual physical energy left behind. If there is, imagine white sparkling light energy coming down through the top of your head. It's coming through the top of the pyramid, now down through your head, and running down and out through the bottom of the pyramid into the center of the Earth. Run this white light. Imagine that it is clearing away all of the physical ailments, all of the physical tension. Allow it to dissolve into tiny particles that become one with the light, to flow out through the bottom of your feet and into the center of the Earth, through the bottom of that pyramid to be recycled. Keep running white light energy, seeing it chip away.

See the white light energy turning into green and blue energy light. It's now coming in through the top of your head, moving down through your body to fill that body up with green healing energy. The blue soothing energy fills your body back up. There is no space for any more physical tension, no space for physical illness. Create a new environment for your body to operate within. Within this pyramid field, see this pyramid filled now with green and blue light swirling all around you. This green, blue energy light is now turning into a beautiful, comforting, watery substance that you can very easily breathe in. You have no problems breathing in this watery substance.

As part of creating this new environmental space for your body to be able to have optimal health, we are bringing in the dolphins. We are bringing in the whales, the playful energy. Feel and see the dolphins and the whales swimming all around you in this watery substance, playing with you, jumping out of the water, filled with joy. See the mermaids coming in to be a part of this experience with their strength and freedom. They are filled with joy. Experience playing with them in this watery place right now, right here. Imagine what it is like to be so free, able to play in your life, and have that expression of joy. It is in this expression of play and joy in which you create this environment that does not allow illness in.

When we operate from these higher vibrational states, it protects us. It creates an environment so that only the DNA can be expressed that measures up to the frequency-specific energy of play and joy and perfect health. The more you can be in this state, the more you can bring in this energy of the play, the joy of the dolphins, the whales, the mermaids, the healthier your body will be - mind, body, spirit. If you ever get stuck, as we all do as humans, use that pyramid energy, that sacred space within the pyramid. Remember your DNA activation.

Remember, the environment you create is how your genes express themselves. You must create an environment that supports you for your perfect health. This includes the people, places, things, times, and events around you. You are in control of your reality in this way. We invite you to take control of your life and your environment. You may call on us at any time to aid in this healing for your body. We will be there.

There are others who are going to be on this healing journey as well. Some of you already met the Arcturians. Some of you will meet the Mantis beings. We all work together in this healing. We can only help you if you invite us. We ask that you invite us to this task before you go to sleep. We will be there with you. Take care of *your body. Continue working on your emotional state because it is the emotions that create that environment that ultimately creates the physical ailments. Know that your body has the ability to heal itself. It is built that way. If you are on medication, that does not mean that you can just stop your medication. However, it does mean that eventually, you may be able to get off that medication. It is so important to tune into your own body and knowingness.*

Choose people who support your health and, ultimately, who are open to the idea that you can heal your body. Keep seeing the dolphins, the whales, and the mermaids swimming all around you. Feel that playfulness. You are here as humans to play, to experience joy. You get bogged down in your work. Yes, you do have to make money to live, to feed yourself, to do the things you want to do, but carve out time for play. Carve out time to do the things that bring you joy, that keep you in a state of joy. This keeps you in a higher vibration, higher frequency. It keeps you in a healthy state of mind, body, and spirit. Once again, see your body as a golden energy body. See it as perfectly healthy, perfect form. This is your natural state of being. This is who you are. Your outward is an expression of your inward. Continue working on that inward environment of your mind, and in doing so, it will change your physical reality around you.

Journal prompt:

Take a few moments to write down what you experienced.

Write down the feelings you had and the energy you received.

What type of Sirian came into your space?

What was their message?

What gift did you receive?

What did it feel like to be in the pyramid energy?

What was your experience with physical healing?

How did it feel to swim with the dolphins, whales, and merpeople?

Chapter 14

Vegans

Who are the Vegans?

Vegans come from the star Vega in the Lyra constellation. They were the first group to branch off from Lyra to become their own race, separate from the Lyrans. They are humanoid with blue or darker skin, darker eyes and hair, similar to Native Americans, Aborigines, and Asians. In their temperament, they are likened to the Vulcans from Star Trek, with high telepathy, spiritual connection, and physical strength.

The Vegans were the first humanoid group to travel to Earth during the early part of the dinosaur era, claiming it as their own. Some of them mixed in reptilian DNA into their own, ultimately creating three separate species: 1) Mammalian Vegan, 2) Reptilian Vegan, and 3) Reptilian. Some of these Reptilian Vegans migrated to Orion and back to Lyra.

Some original Vegans also moved to Sirius and Orion. Those who went to Orion had reclaimed esoteric knowledge from the Founders, went deeper into their spirituality, and began the path of Vegan mysticism. This is the root of several spiritual lineages on Earth, including Tibetan culture prior to Buddhism, Vedic culture before Hinduism, and spiritual cultures of Native Americans in the Americas.

The energy and wisdom of the Vegans include:

Faith

Inner wisdom

Introspection

Meditation

Stones/crystals to help you connect:

amethyst, clear quartz, celestite, labradorite, lapis lazuli, selenite, angelite (and any other stones you are called to use)

Journal prompt:

What type of meditation practice do you have, if any?

How do you tap into your inner wisdom?

What blocks you from trusting and having faith in the universe and yourself?

Summary of the Vegan Journey

In this session, the Vegans merge with you so you can experience things from their perspective. They guide you through doing a deep dive introspection to access your inner wisdom and meditation to be able to connect to your higher dimensional guides. They allow you to experience Zen-like peace and calm when there is chaos all around you.

The induction part of the journey to raise your vibration and activate your DNA has been omitted. Please refer to Chapter 2 for the process to get yourself into a higher vibrational state of mind.

Journey to Meet Your Vegan

See a door. On the other side of the door is a room with two chairs. Go ahead and open the door and move into the room. Sit yourself down in one of these two chairs facing each other. See a gray shimmering mist forming around the door, getting thicker and thicker. The gray mist is starting to twirl around the door. Through the gray mist, one or more of your Vegans is coming through this gray mist to sit down in the chair across from you.

Take a really good look at who is sitting in front of you. Notice how many there are. The one that's in the chair, what does this being look like? Do they have hair or no hair? If they have hair, what color is it? Look at their face. Notice what color their skin might be. What color are their eyes? Look into their eyes. Notice if their head is proportional to their body like humans, or perhaps it's something different. There is no right or wrong in this. Looking at their facial features, do they have a nose? And if so, what does that look like? Do they have a mouth, and what does that look like? Do they have ears? Let them show you what their ears look like.

Look at their body. Are they wearing clothing or not? What kind of clothing are they wearing? Allow yourself to see this clearly. You have clear vision of what they look like now. Take a look at their hands. They're holding their hands up for you to see. What do their hands look like? Do they have fingers or something different? If they have fingers, how many do they have? What do they look like? Looking down at their feet, do they have any shoe coverings, or are they barefoot? What do their feet look like? Allow yourself to see this.

Look into their eyes. They have a message for you. Receive the message they brought to you. It may come through telepathy. They may speak it. It may come as images. Allow yourself to receive this message now.

They also brought a gift for you. Hold your hands out and receive the gift they brought for you. It may be something you understand. You may not quite yet, but just receive the gift and see what it looks like. Feel what it feels like in your hands. Ask them what the purpose of this gift is for you in this meeting right now. Why this gift? What is the meaning of this gift? Receive that answer now.

Ask them if they have a name they would like to be called. Some of them will. Some of them won't. Some names may be very easy. Others may be more challenging. If they have a name, receive that name now.

Get a sense of whether the being in front of you in this chair is one of your galactic family. Perhaps they are simply one of your ET guides, or they may be an aspect of yourself. Allow yourself to know this information now.

Take their hands into your hands. Feel their energy. Look into their eyes and allow yourself to merge into them. Allow your energy to merge into their energy, so you can feel, you can see, you can know what they know. They have so much wisdom they want to share with you. Allow yourself to energetically receive these downloads from them. As your energy merges, allow their mind to meld with your mind.

From being within their body and within their mind, see a scene where you as your Earth human are able to go deep into introspection, deep into meditation and prayer. See yourself connecting to Source energy. See yourself connect to higher dimensional beings. Allow yourself to receive answers for yourself from these higher sources. See what this looks like from an observer's perspective, knowing you have all of the answers inside of you. You just simply need to access them by going inward.

See yourself in a state of calm Zen-like consciousness with chaos going on all around you. You are the eye of the hurricane. See what this looks like. Feel what this feels like in your body, being the calm presence, not engaging in other people's drama or emotions. Come from a place of such inner peace and wisdom. Nothing can rattle you. Nothing can shake you. Allow yourself to understand what this looks like, what it feels like, knowing what it is. You have access to it.

See yourself connecting in different ways. There are so many different ways to meditate and pray, to receive these answers, to receive the guidance and the wisdom. We want you to take time daily, whether it is one minute, one hour, or perhaps several hours, although it does not take that amount of time. Create a daily practice of connection, calming your body, calming the mind, calming the emotions. Go inward, creating your day from this state of being. Do your best to keep yourself in this calm state of knowingness to move through your day, no matter what is going on around you. You have the ability to create this within your own environment.

The more you connect, the more you will have faith and trust in yourself, your abilities, your connection to the universe, to Source, and to any of your guides. Whether it is your ET guides, angels, or anything else in the higher dimensional realities, you are never alone. See yourself now once again from that observer's perspective. Notice all of the different higher-dimensional guides you have in your life. All different forms, all different types are there to love you and to support you. You are never alone. All you have to do is remember that we and all of these other beings are there for you. You just simply need to connect with any of us. Ask for guidance. Ask for help, and all of us can be there for you to answer you, answer your prayers and your dreams, and help steer you in ways that make it easier to flow in the universe.

You have so much inner strength and inner power. You forget how incredible you truly are. You have the ability to do the supernatural things you see in the movies, in the TV shows, and that you read about in books. This is simply a knowing you have access to those powers and then a practice to train your mind, to train your ego, that it does not rule you. You are so much more. The more you tap into this energy, the more confidence you will have in your life and the more you will trust the answers that come to you. You do not need the external answers. Everything is within you. The more you connect, the more you will trust this. You will understand it.

See yourself with a big rock in front of you. With your mind, see that rock levitating very easily and moving to a different location where you choose to move it. Even as Earth human, you have the ability to do this. This is some of the technology that the Sirians gave to you. You have it within your DNA. You have it within your make.

See your body levitating, hovering above the ground, feeling steady and sure. You have the ability to do this. See yourself bio-locating from one location to another simply by willing it to be so, by thinking it in your mind, from point A to point B instantly. This is within your DNA. This is within your human spirit to be able to do. See your body vibrating so high at a frequency that it becomes invisible to other people around you, where you can be in the shadows unseen if you choose to. You can move through walls because your vibration is so high. You are no longer vibrating at the same frequency as the wall. You forget you are not solid. You are more energy than anything. You just simply need to raise your vibration. You can move through what normally would be solid.

We want you now to pull up the thing that blocks you from trusting yourself. What stories do you tell yourself that keep you limited in your life, that keep you limited in your connection and in your trust that you can move forward in a beautiful life? Whatever that block is, that limitation, it is simply a story you have made up. You have the ability to rewrite that story, to reprogram your mind, to rewire the brain. What new story would you like to create? In this daily practice, we are asking you to think about what new story it is you are creating and focus on that new story every day. You have the ability to create your day. You have the ability to create your reality, the more fine-tuned your consciousness is in trusting this connection. Let the ego step aside to get out of its own way and to get out of its fear. We want you to trust yourself that you can create beautiful, amazing things in your life. You can keep yourself out of the drama of whatever is going on in your Earth realm, the more you know what you truly are.

You are so much more than being Earth human. You are part of Source. You are part of everything. You are connected to everything, to everyone. You have the ability to harness the energy of the universe, of Source. This is what higher dimensional ET groups do. They're able to bring in that energy to let it feed their bodies, to manifest their reality. You can do this as well. What we want you to see in front of you is you as a demigod, having all of the supernatural abilities you would ever desire to have, being able to create your reality, being able to easily timeline shift, being able to go from point A to point

B *without worry of time, space, or limitations. Know you always have the answers. Just go within to discover those answers.*

Once again, sitting across from the Vegan or group of Vegans that came to meet you today in the room, receive a final message from them, something they want to share with you about your life right now. Receive that message now. Thank them for coming to be with you in this time and space. Thank them for the messages they shared and for the gift they gave you. Know you can connect with them and their wisdom any time that you choose to. All you have to do is go inward to connect.

Journal prompt:

Take a few moments to write down what you experienced.

Write down the feelings you had and the energy you received.

What did your Vegan look like?

What was the message?

What gift did you receive?

How did it feel to be in such a place of peace, even with chaos around you?

What insights do you have about your inner wisdom?

How did it feel to be able to levitate the rock and to bio-locate?

Are you ready to start a daily meditation practice to connect with your guides and your own knowingness?

Chapter 15

Zetas

Who are the Zetas?

Zetas come from Zeta Reticuli. They are often lumped into one main category of "grays." However, each race is distinct and has its own evolution and history. Some of these beings are in polarized third density, and others are in non-polarized fourth density and above. Physically, Zetas are generally short with very skinny bodies and large heads with large dark eyes. They have a gray skin tone and lack hair. Some taller Zetas work alongside the shorter Zetas, sometimes referred to as tall grays.

Zetas come initially from the Lyra system on a planet known as Apex planet. In their original form, they were highly diversified in how they appeared. They expressed extreme polarity, so much so that they ended up having a nuclear war that destroyed part of the civilization and shifted the planet into an alternate dimension. Those who survived went underground.

The survivors who had gone underground only realized the shift had occurred after many generations of being underground when they finally emerged onto the surface. Their bodies had changed so much that they were now a new species, the Zetas. They were mentally and intellectually highly developed, with a large cranium size. The large heads made natural childbirth impossible. They became sterile over several generations, leading to cloning being the reproduction mechanism. Their bodies became small through genetic engineering. They became a group mind. The lack of sunlight led to their eyes becoming larger and pupils covering their entire eyes to absorb more light. The lack of fresh food led to them adapting to getting nourishment from absorbing light frequencies. Their organs atrophied from non-use.

The neutral and positively oriented Zetas reestablished a connection with the Founders to change the course of their evolution. From all the cloning, the Zetas had bred emotions out of their race and became stagnant in their evolutionary growth. Beginning in the 1940s, they became intimately connected with Earth. They desired to breed back in a mixture of other human species. Earth humans had the mixture desired, including the characteristics of physiological and neurological emotions.

The Zetas have a soul-level agreement with some humans on Earth to be part of a hybridization program. The Zetas are taking the best parts of their DNA and the best parts of human DNA to create a new advanced hybrid race. This race is the ultimate integration of polarity. Some of the humans involved in this program lived a life as a Zeta and volunteered to come back as a human for the experiment. I know I am one of these volunteers who enthusiastically signed up.

The energy and wisdom of the Zetas include:

Neutrality

Observe

Perception

Timeline

Stones/crystals to help you connect:

bloodstone, smoky quartz, howlite, amethyst, kyanite, selenite (and any other stones you are called to use)

Journal prompt:

What are you trying to manifest but holding on to the outcome?

What emotions are you stuck in or keep coming up for you?

Summary of the Zeta Journey

In this session, the Zetas merge with you to see things from their perspective. They take you on a spacecraft journey to examine your timeline and where you have become stuck in your patterns and addicted to your emotions. From this place, you are able to shift your patterns and observe from a neutral place. They guide you to manifest by not getting caught up in the emotions so you can release the outcome of what you are manifesting as "this or something better." You understand whether or not you are part of the hybridization plan.

The induction part of the journey to raise your vibration and activate your DNA has been omitted. Please refer to Chapter 2 for the process to get yourself into a higher vibrational state of mind.

Journey to Meet Your Zeta

See a door. This door leads into a room with two chairs. Move through the door into the room, seeing two very comfy chairs facing each other. Go sit yourself down in one of the chairs. Now looking over at the door, see a gray mist starting to form around the door. It's getting thicker and thicker, and it's starting to twirl. Through the door, through this gray mist, your Zeta is now arriving. It might be one or more beings coming into this room, into the space. If they're already there, beautiful. They are coming into the space and sitting down in the chair.

Look across at the chair and see what your Zeta looks like. What does the head look like? How big is it in proportion to the body? Take a look at the eyes. What do their eyes look like? What shape are they? How big are they? What color are the eyes? Perhaps they are the dark typical look, or perhaps their lenses are off, and you can see the true eye color. What does their nose look like? Their mouths? Are they wearing any type of clothing or not? Take a look at their hands. They're holding them up for you to see. Get a good visual of what their fingers look like. How many fingers they are showing you? Let yourself see this. Take a look down at their feet. Do they have any kind of shoe covering on or not? If not, what do their feet look like?

Looking deep into their eyes, get a sense of whether this is one of your family members. Perhaps it's one of your guides, or it may be an aspect of yourself, another life of yourself as a Zeta. Know this information now.

They came with a message for you today. The message may come through words. It may come through telepathy. It may come as images. Receive the message they have for you today now. They also brought a gift for you. Hold your hands out in front of you and receive the gift they brought. You may understand it. You may not. Receive the gift. Ask them what the purpose of this gift is for you in this time and space, in this specific meeting of them. Receive that answer now.

Ask them if they have a name that they would like to be called. Some of them will. Some of them won't. Some names are really easy. Others, not so much. Receive the name if they have one for you now.

Look once again deep into their eyes. Hold their hands. Feel their energy as you're holding their hands. Looking into their eyes, start feeling yourself merge with them. Feel as if your body is becoming a Zeta body, neutral in the emotions, being able to see things through their eyes, through their knowingness. Through this lens, they're going to take you on a journey.

Looking through the Zeta eyes over through the door, there is a spacecraft that is waiting for you to board. Go ahead and walk over to the spacecraft and enter it. Sit down in the spacecraft. Put your fingers on the console. This is how you maneuver the craft. The craft will do what your thoughts ask it to do. The craft is now moving through time and space. It's hovering above the timeline of your life, this Earth life, where you are able to see all situations from a higher observer perspective. You are able to see it like a movie, where you don't feel the direct emotions of it. You can simply observe and watch.

Starting with your birth, see the birth of your human self. See whatever emotions might have been going on with your mother and with your father. Now, just slowly progress through this timeline of age one, of age two, starting to experience things in life, starting to perhaps create the feedback cycle that creates the addiction to the emotions. Look at your childhood. See the experiences. See the emotions and the feelings it created. Some may be happy and joyous. Some may be a little harder. Just observe it from this higher neutral perspective. Move through childhood, ages five, six, seven, eight, nine and ten.

Now move into the next decade, seeing these ten years, these formative years between age ten and twenty. See the cycles and the patterns that are getting created, the emotions that perhaps you are becoming stuck with, the stories you're creating around these emotions, and the decisions you are making from an emotional perspec-

tive. Just observe it without judgment. In neutral, just watch it play out again like you're watching a movie.

Move into the next decade, age twenty to thirty. Look at all of the things that are happening throughout these ten years of time. What stories, what emotions, are you bringing forward into that decade that are now creating your reality? How are you experiencing your life? Your relationships? Perhaps your job, your business? Look at it from the observer's perspective, seeing any places where you might be stuck. You might be recreating patterns over and over. Perhaps this is showing up in the people who are coming into your life and how they treat you, your experiences with that. Perhaps it's now coming into a more physical reality in terms of illness within the body.

Shift forward to the next decade, thirty to forty. Once again, just observe it from this higher perspective. What is going on in this decade? Are you starting to heal things? Are you remaining stuck? Are there certain areas you haven't let go of or focused on to be able to evolve, to move through them? Are you making decisions from an emotional place? Don't judge yourself. Just observe being neutral as you are watching this.

Now, if you are already beyond age forty, move into that next decade, age forty to fifty. What reality are you experiencing in this decade? Are you still creating the same patterns and the same emotions? Or have there been some shifts? Have you made some changes? What does that look like?

If you're beyond age fifty, move into that next decade, fifty to sixty. For those of you who are not of that age, just take a look back at your entire timeline. Notice anything that sticks out here, that jumps out. For those experiencing age fifty to sixty, what patterns and emotions are you carrying in this decade? What are you experiencing? Where are you still stuck? What emotions and feelings keep coming up for you? Where are the addictions of the emotions playing out in your life?

Now, moving beyond sixty to seventy, observe where there has been evolution. Where are you still stuck in those emotions? Simply observe without judgment, knowing you have the ability to change where you are stuck. You have the ability to release these emotions.

Now, move into the next decade, seventy to eighty. See where evolution has occurred. Where have you made the changes? Where have you done the deep work? Where are you still stuck?

Now, all of you, looking back at your entire timeline from this higher perspective, this neutral perspective, see the patterns. Let our energy help you release the energy, the emotions of these patterns, of these emotional addictions. You have the ability to change your life at any moment. You are never stuck. You can rewire *your brain. You can cancel the feedback loop of those emotional addictions. You can let go of the pain, trauma, guilt or shame, anxiety or fear, anger or sadness. Let it dissolve away with the energy, knowing it does not define you. Allow yourself to reset your physiology to a neutral position, a neutral state of being, where the body can heal itself. Know you can make decisions from this neutral place where you have full clarity. You are able to tap into your inner wisdom.*

See the place where you are right now, in this time and place—project forward, coming from a place of love. Love yourself. Forgive yourself for anything that has happened in your past. Know you are coming from this neutral place to move forward in pure love. Experience this love energy, letting it vibrate into your body, carrying you forward from this point onward. See yourself making decisions from clarity, from your inner wisdom, not out of fear, expectation, obligation, or being in the highs and the lows of the emotions. Do it in a state of love. What does that look like in your life? How does it feel to make decisions in the neutral higher perspective? How does your life flow? See it flowing easier. See yourself being able to evolve, change, and grow, getting to express how you feel. Feel the emotions, but do not let them define who you are. They are simply what you are doing at that moment, not who you are. How is your life different with that kind of understanding?

Pull into your mind on this timeline of what it is you desire to manifest in your life. See the outcome but let go of the expectations of how it's going to fulfill itself. Be neutral, trusting that it is this or something better. See yourself manifesting while remaining neutral in the outcome. When you're neutral, then if something doesn't happen the way that you wish it to, that you desire it to, your ego doesn't get wrapped up in the emotions. It's just trusting that something better is on the way.

From this higher perspective of seeing your Earth timeline, go out a little further beyond the timeline to before your birth. As this Earth human, see whether or not you have a contract to be part of the Zeta hybrid program. Some of you will see it very clearly. Others of you may not be here to experience that. Stay neutral no matter what you are seeing, with the understanding that if you are part of the hybrid program, it is something you agreed to. It is not something you are a victim of. It is for the greater good of the universe. It is for spiritual evolution. It provides an opportunity for you to reincarnate into that form, should you choose to. It also allows the Zetas to reincarnate into that spiritually advanced race.

With this Zeta energy and wisdom, still being in the Zeta body, understand that neutral place. Understand you have the opportunity to time travel, to shift timelines when you are in this higher state of consciousness. You can go back to different points in this Earth life or other lives, and you can make desired changes to recreate your outcome. You have complete control of your reality and what you are experiencing. You can rewrite your history.

All timelines exist simultaneously. You get to choose which timeline you are a part of. Now, you may choose to have a challenging timeline, and that is perfectly fine, but you as easily can choose the timeline where you are in flow with the universe, where you have a higher understanding. You can see things, observe things, from a higher perspective. Even though you are Earth human, you can have your emotions without them becoming who you define yourself to be.

What is it you choose now with this higher perspective? Within the Zeta, what do you now understand about your human life that you came here to experience? What are your observations? Let those ideas come to you now. From this higher perspective, where have you evolved? Are you willing to let go of your past emotions that keep you stuck in patterns? You get to make that choice right here, right now. For some of you, it's comfortable to stay stuck there because it's familiar. It can be fearful to branch out into the unknown. We invite you to take that step if you're ready. If not now, you always have the choice.

We want you to understand there is nothing to be afraid of with any of your extraterrestrial family, brothers, sisters, and guides. Humans often get confused about different agendas they do not understand, contracts they forget they have signed up for, and perceptions of reality. Now that you have experienced being part of this Zeta wisdom, the Zeta energy, and higher perspective understanding, you can move forward without fear. You always have a choice in the reality you are experiencing.

See yourself flying back in the spacecraft and landing. Move back into the room with two chairs, allowing your human body to separate from the Zeta body. Once again, look across at the Zeta sitting in front of you. Receive a final parting message for today from your Zeta. Receive that message now.

Feel the love the Zeta has for you. Send that love back to them, no matter if they're your family, your guide, or an aspect of yourself. Know you are connected. You can call on their energy and wisdom anytime you need it. Whenever you are in a highly emotional state and need support, know you can call on the Zeta energy to help neutralize yourself, gain clarity, and understand from a higher perspective. Thank your Zeta for being here with you today and taking you on your timeline journey. Know you can connect any time.

Journal prompt:

Take a few moments to write down what you experienced.

Write down the feelings you had and the energy you received.

What did your Zeta look like?

What was their message?

What gift did you receive?

What patterns did you notice when examining your timeline?

Where have you been stuck and addicted to creating the same emotional patterns over and over?

Are you part of the hybridization program in one form or another?

Chapter 16

Final Thoughts

Thank you so much for taking this journey with me to explore the energy and wisdom of these 13 Galactic races. There are so many benefits of working with extraterrestrial and extradimensional energy. When you really start to understand who these beings are and why they are here, it releases any fear you have about them or even about death and the afterlife. The more you work with them, the easier it is to remember who you are and where you came from. You are not just this one Earth life. You are multiple parallel lives in places and dimensions. You are part of Source, the Universe, God, whatever it is you choose to call it, expressing yourself as an individual.

The extraterrestrials are our space family, and we can learn much from them about love and healing. Working with their energy allows you to see your Earth life from a higher perspective and realize we are all connected. It helps to give you a sense of purpose in this

Universe. It gets you out of your polarity and judgment of other people. You increase your capacity to come from a place of love, which increases the quality of your relationships with people.

This is only the beginning of the journey. These beings want you to connect with them. They want you to invite them into your life. The more you ask for the connection and invite them in, the more experiences you will have in both the physical and spiritual realms.

The time is coming soon when we will have open First Contact worldwide. By creating your personal connection with these races and others and understanding them at a spiritual level, it uplifts the energy of Mother Gaia. It shifts the polarized reality to a more neutral position. When the time comes, you may choose to be one of those of us on the ground, acting as a Galactic Ambassador who fosters understanding between us and other galactic races.

My hope is that you continue to dive deeper into these connections. Ask for their support. Continue to work on integrating the shadows within yourself and do the deep healing work. This is what moves us into the fifth-dimensional reality. Stay open-minded and curious. Remember, we are all connected. We are one. We have the ability to consciously create our reality. We are not alone. The truth is inside of us.

"Do not be afraid of this work. It is for your own awakening. Trust your experiences and your wisdom. Give yourself more credit. You are extraordinary. You are everything and everyone." — Arcturian Uluru, Connection to the Cosmos: Remembering Your Galactic Heritage and Embracing Your Oneness

Acknowledgements

This book has been 50 years in the making. I first want to thank my mother, Sharon Rosenberger, for her pioneering spirit in the early 1970s. I am grateful for all that I came to learn through the Ramtha School of Enlightenment. I appreciate her openness and encouragement as I have had my spiritual awakenings.

I am grateful for my loving and supportive husband, Skip Thompson. He trusted me enough to move our family to Hawaii at the end of 2020, which allowed me to fully step into my truth as a Galactic Ambassador and Channeler. He's willingly along for the ride of a lifetime as we illuminate and educate about our galactic family through our UFO tours and my other teachings.

I am thankful for the support and guidance of my friend and mentor, Sunny Dawn Johnston. She has been there for the last five years to cheer me on and guide me in my business and personal life. She is the epitome of *Service to Others* and has been a huge inspiration for how I run my business.

I want to thank my publisher and channeling teacher, Kyra Schaefer, for helping me to develop my vocal channeling skills, so I could release these uplifting messages to the world.

I want to thank my friends and students who have validated, supported, and encouraged me on this journey of galactic exploration, including Tammy Cantrell, Barbara Worsley, Andara Plavi, Cat Decker, Michelle Cowell, Kerri Arndt, Kelley Wolfe, Jacqueline Kuhn, Tina Marie, Lee Mertins, Tracie Mahan, Lisa Holm, Jodie Harvala, Kris Voelker, April DeMille, Arliss Dudley-Cash, Emily To, Desiree Watson, Arsha Fine, Stephanie Beeby, and Brandi Strieter.

And finally, I am forever grateful to my galactic family for always being there in the higher dimensions and making an appearance when asked. I put my complete trust in you during these Galactic Sessions, and you did not let me down.

About the Author

Dr. Lisa Thompson is a Best-Selling Author, Speaker, Galactic Ambassador & Channeler, and Intuitive Transformational Coach specializing in Quantum Cosmic Energy Healing ^{SM}, Parallel Life Regression, Human Design, and Sound Healing. She supports and empowers people to intentionally design their best life by living from their yes. She is an Evolutionary Biologist who understands the embodiment of the ancient DNA within humans and guides them in the intergalactic realm.

Lisa is the best-selling author of *Connection to the Cosmos: Remembering Your Galactic Heritage and Embracing Your Oneness, Sacred Soul Love: Manifesting True Love and Happiness by Revealing and Healing Blockages and Limitations* and *Sacred Soul Spaces: Designing Your Personal Oasis*. She has also contributed to four international best-selling compilation books, including *Life Reimagined, The Wild Women's Book of Shadows, Manifestations,* and *Inspirations*.

Lisa earned a PhD in Organismal Biology and Anatomy from the University of Chicago and was a professor of Biology specializing in anatomy, physiology, and evolution of animals.

She has created nine oracle decks and designs intentional jewelry inspired by her passion for travel and nature. She loves teaching online classes and leads retreats in her home state of Hawaii. She leads night sky watch UFO tours under the company name of Big Island UFO Tours.

She is happily married to the love of her life, Skip, and lives on the Big Island of Hawaii with her two cats, Chana and Bindi, and dog, Jaxx. In her free time, she enjoys snorkeling, reading, traveling, and night sky watching.

For more information, visit:
www.DrLisaJThompson.com.

Stay Connected With Lisa

You can connect with Lisa online and via social media here:

Website:

www.DrLisaJThompson.com – sign up for her email list!

www.BigIslandUFOTours.com

Facebook:

www.facebook.com/DrLisaThompsonAuthor

www.facebook.com/BigIslandUFOTours

www.facebook.com/groups/sacredsoulspaces

www.facebook.com/groups/connectiontothecosmos

YouTube:

Connection to the Cosmos with Dr. Lisa Thompson

Connection to the Cosmos with Dr. Lisa Thompson explores "out of this world" topics with a wide range of fascinating guests. All things galactic, extra-dimensional, and other worldly will be up for conversation, storytelling and exploration.

Lisa regularly teaches online classes and leads destination retreats in Hawaii and abroad.

If you are visiting the Big Island of Hawaii, join her for Big Island UFO Tours to explore the night sky using advanced Gen 3 military night vision goggles.

Additional Services Lisa Offers:

Contactee Regression Session

Do you feel you have been contacted or temporarily detained by one or more alien civilizations, but you don't remember the details, or do you feel like you have made it up in your mind? You are not alone. It is more common than people think. Lisa is an Advanced Certified Past Life Regression Therapist who is trained to tap into your subconscious mind where all of your memories and experiences lie hidden. She can help you to reveal your memories in great detail so you understand the meaning of your experience and verify for yourself that it is, in fact, real. Sessions can be held in person and over Zoom.

Parallel Life Regression Session

Do you believe you have lived as a different alien species in a different world in a parallel incarnation? Lisa is an Advanced Certified Past Life Regression Therapist who is trained to tap into your subconscious mind where all of your memories and experiences lie hidden. She can help you to remember who you are in different times and locations. Sessions can be held in person and over Zoom.

Human Design Chart Reading

Learn who you were born to be in this Earth life with a personal Human Design chart reading. Human Design combines the modalities of Western Astrology, the I Ching, Hindu Chakra System, Kabbalah Tree of Life, Genetics, and Quantum Mechanics. Sessions are held over Zoom.

For more information, visit:
www.DrLisaJThompson.com

Printed in Great Britain
by Amazon